Little Red Book
of
Antonyms

Other Titles in the Series

Little Red Book of SMS Slang and Chat Room Slang	Little Red Book of Synonyms
Little Red Book of English Vocabulary Today	Little Red Book of Common Errors
	Little Red Book of Letter Writing
Little Red Book of Grammar Made Easy	Little Red Book of Essay Writing
	Little Red Book of Word Fact
Little Red Book of English Proverbs	Little Red Book of Spelling
	Little Red Book of Language Checklist
Little Red Book of Prepositions	
Little Red Book of Idioms and Phrases	Little Red Book of Perfect Written English
Little Red Book of Effective Speaking Skills	Little Red Book of Punctuation
	Little Red Book of Reading and Listening Skills
Little Red Book of Phrasal Verbs	
Little Red Book of Euphemisms	Little Red Book of A Child's First Dictionary
Little Red Book of Word Power	
Little Red Book of Modern Writing Skills	Little Red Book of Phonics

Little Red Book *of* Antonyms

Terry O'Brien

RUPA

Published by
Rupa Publications India Pvt. Ltd 2012
7/16, Ansari Road, Daryaganj
New Delhi 110002

Sales centres:
Prayagraj Bengaluru Chennai
Hyderabad Jaipur Kathmandu
Kolkata Mumbai

Copyright © Terry O'Brien 2012

All rights reserved.
No part of this publication may be reproduced, transmitted,
or stored in a retrieval system, in any form or by any means,
electronic, mechanical, photocopying, recording or otherwise,
without the prior permission of the publisher.

P-ISBN: 978-81-291-1968-1
E-ISBN: 978-81-291-4392-1

Tenth impression 2023

15 14 13 12 11 10

The moral right of the author has been asserted.

Typeset by Innovative Processors, Delhi

Printed in India

This book is sold subject to the condition that it shall not, by way
of trade or otherwise, be lent, resold, hired out, or otherwise circulated,
without the publisher's prior consent, in any form of binding or cover
other than that in which it is published.

*I dedicate this book to late Prof. A.P. O'Brien,
my father, friend, guide and mentor, who
inspired me to the canon of excellence:
re-imagining what's essential*

PREFACE

ANTONYMS: A word having a meaning opposite to that of another word: *The word* wet *is an antonym of the word* dry. *Cold* and *hot* are antonyms; so are *small* and *large*. **In Brief:** An antonym is a word with an opposite meaning to another word. *The antonym to the word "good" is "bad."*

In Lexical semantics, **opposites** are words that lie in an inherently incompatible binary relationship as in the opposite pairs– *male: female*, *long : short*, *up : down*, and *precede : follow*. For example, something that is *long* entails that it is not *short*. It is referred to as a 'binary' relationship because there are two members in a set of opposites. The relationship between opposites is known as **opposition**. A member of a pair of opposites can generally be determined by the question *What is the opposite of X ?*

The term **antonym** (and the related **antonymy**) has also been commonly used as a term that is synonymous with *opposite*; however, the term also has other more restricted meanings. One usage has *antonym* referring to both gradable opposites, such as *long : short*, and (non-gradable) complementary opposites, such as *male : female*, while opposites of the types *up: down*.

A third usage defines the term *antonym* as referring to only gradable opposites (the *long : short* type) while the other types are referred to with different terms.

Happy reading

Dr Terry O'Brien

Antonyms

A

Abandon vb.	join, engage, unite, embrace, retain
Abandoned adj.	righteous, virtuous
Abate vb.	increase
Abbreviate vb.	lengthen, extend, augment
Abbreviation n.	extension
Abduct vb.	restore
Aberrant n.	regular
Abet vb.	oppose
Aberration n.	regularity
Abeyance n.	revival
Abhor vb.	adore
Abhorrence adj.	adorable
Abide vb.	perish, depart, break
Abject adj.	honourable
Adjure vb.	acknowledge
Able adj.	unable, incompetent, incapable
Abnormal adj.	normal, average, usual
Abnormality n.	normality
Abolish vb.	establish, retain
Abominable adj.	admirable, fine, noble, loveable
Abominate vb.	adore, love
Aboriginal n.	alien

Abort vb.	achieve
Abound vb.	lack
Abortive adj.	successful
About adv.	precisely
Above prep.	below, under
Above	beneath
Abridge vb.	expand, extend, increase
Abridgement n.	extenstion
Abroad adv.	privately, secretely
Abrogate vb.	enact
Abrupt adj.	gradual, courteous
Abscond vb.	appear
Absence n.	presence, existence
Absent n.	present, attentive
Absentminded adj.	alert, attentive
Absolute adj.	partial, limited, fragmentary, incomplete, dubious
Absolutely adv.	uncertainly, doubtfully, partially
Absolution n.	condemnation
Absolve vb.	accuse, charge
Absorb vb.	leak, drain, exude
Absorbent adj.	impermeable
Absorbing adj.	dull
Abstain vb.	indulge
Abstemious adj.	greedy
Abstinence n.	self-indulgence

Abstract adj.	concrete **vb.** unite, expand
Abstracted adj.	attentive
Abstraction n.	attention, union
Abstruse adj.	clear
Absurd adj.	sensible, sound, reasonable
Abundance n.	scarcity, want, dearth, absence
Abundant adj.	scarce, rare, uncommon, absent
Abuse vb. n.	praise
Abusive adj.	complimentary
Accede vb.	disagree
Accelerate vb.	retard
Accept vb.	refuse, reject, ignore, repudiate
Acceptable adj.	unacceptable, unwelcome
Acceptance n.	refusal
Accepted adj.	unconventional
Accessible adj.	inaccessible, unavailable, unapproachable, not reachable, unfriendly
Accession adj.	decrease
Accessory n.	essential **vb.** chief
Accidental adj.	planned, international, deliberate, on purpose
Acclaim vb.	denounce
Acclamation n.	denunciation
Accommodate vb.	inconvenience, disoblige

Accommodating adj.	unfriendly
Accompany vb.	abandon, leave, forsake, desert
Accomplice n.	opponent
Accomplish vb.	fail
Accomplished adj.	unskilled
Accomplishment n.	failure
Accord n.	disagreement, difference, quarrel, discord **vb.**
Accordance n.	difference
Accordant adj.	discordant
Accost vb.	avoid
Accretion n.	dispersion
Accrue vb.	diminish
Accumulate vb.	disperse
Accumulation n.	dispersion
Accurate adj.	inaccurate, inexact, mistaken, wrong
Accursed adj.	blessed
Accusation n.	vindication
Accuse vb.	absolve, exculpate, clear
Accuser n.	defendant
Accustomed adj.	unfamiliar, strange, unusual
Acerbity n.	sweetness
Achieve vb.	fail

Achievement n.	failure
Acid adj.	sweet, mild, bland
Acknowledge vb.	deny, refuse, reject
Acknowledgement n.	ignore, denial
Acme n.	base
Acquainted adj.	ignorant
Acquiesce vb.	object
Acquiescence n.	objection
Acquire vb.	lose, forfeit
Acquisition n.	loss
Acquit vb.	condemn, sentence
Acrid adj.	sweet
Acrimonious adj.	amicable
Acrimony n.	mildness
Action n.	inaction
Active adj.	lazy, inactive, lethargic, indolent, sluggish
Activity n.	idleness, inactivity
Actual adj.	unreal, false, fake, bogus, pretended
Actuate vb.	deter
Acumen n.	stupidity
Acute adj.	obtuse, insensitive, mild, bland
Adamant adj.	flexible
Adaptable adj.	inflexible, rigid
Add vb.	subtract, remove, withdraw

Addition n.	decrease
Address vb.	ignore
Adept adj.	incompetent
Adequate adj.	inadequate, insufficient
Adhere vb.	separate, loosen
Adherent adj.	defector, renegade, dropout
Adjacent adj.	apart, distant, separate
Adjoin vb.	separate
Adjoining adj.	separate, distant, remote
Adjourn vb.	assemble, convene, begin, complete
Adjunct adj.	essential
Admirable adj.	contemptible, despicable, sorry
Admiration n.	contempt, disdain, disrespect
Admire vb.	dislike, loathe, detest, hate, despise
Admissible adj.	inadmissible
Admission n.	denial, exclusion
Admit vb.	deny, obstruct, reject, exclude
Admittance n.	exclusion
Admonish vb.	praise, glorify, commend
Admonition n.	praise, comment, glorify
Ado n.	tranquility, quietude
Adolescence n.	maturity
Adolescent n.	adult **adj.** grown, mature
Adopt vb.	abandon, reject
Adorable adj.	abominable, despicable
Adoration n.	abomination, hatred

Adore vb.	despise, hate, loathe
Adorn vb.	strip, bare
Adrift adj.	secure, well-organized, purposeful, stable
Adroit adj.	clumsy, awkward, oafish, graceless
Adulation n.	obloquy
Adult n.	child **adj.** immature, infantile
Adulterate vb.	purify
Adulterated adj.	pure
Adultery n.	fidelity
Advance vb.	retreat, withdraw, flee, retard, obstruct **n.** retreat, withdrawl, retardation
Adumbrate vb.	reveal
Advantage n.	disadvantage, hindrance, loss
Advantageous adj.	prejudicial
Advent n.	departure
Adventurous adj.	timid
Adversary n.	friend, ally
Adverse adj.	favourable, beneficial
Adversity n.	happiness, prosperity, benefit
Adversity vb.	conceal, suppress
Advisable adj.	inadvisable, ill-considered, imprudent
Advise vb.	deter
Aesthetic adj.	tasteless, ugly

Advocate vb.	oppose n. opponent, foe, adversary
Advocacy n.	opposition
Afar adj.	nearby
Affable adj.	haughty
Affectation n.	natural, unaffected, genuine
Affection n.	dislike, aversion, antipathy
Affectionate adj.	cold, distant, unfeeling
Affiliate vb.	sever
Affliation n.	severance
Affinity n.	antipathy
Affirm vb.	deny, disclaim
Affirmation n.	denial
Affirmative adj.	negative
Affix vb.	detach
Afflict vb.	console
Affliction n.	benefit, comfort, relief, easement
Affluence n.	poverty
Affluent adj.	scarce
Affray n.	order
Affront vb.	pacify
Afire vb.	extinguished, indifferent
Afraid adj.	bold, courageous, confident
After prep.	before
Afterwards adv.	before
Against prep.	for, in favour of, pro, in support of, with

Aged adj.	young, youthful
Agglomerate vb.	disperse
Aggravate vb.	ease, relief, soothe
Aggravation n.	mitigation
Aggregate vb.	disperse **n.** unit
Aggregation vb.	distribution
Aggression n.	resistance, passivity
Aggressive adj.	passive, shy, timid, withdrawn
Aggrieve vb.	soothe
Aghast adj.	relieved
Agile adj.	clumsy, awkward, inept
Agility n.	clumsiness
Agitate vb.	calm, soothe
Agitated adj.	calm, composed
Agitation n.	calmness
Agnostic adj.	believer
Agonize vb.	soothe
Agony n.	ecstasy
Agree vb.	disagree, argue, refuse, differ
Agreeable adj.	disagreeable, quarrelsome, contentious, touchy
Agreement n.	disagreement, discord, misunderstanding
Aground vb.	afloat
Ahead adv.	impede, obstruct, hinder **n.** obstacle, hindrance, opponent
Ailing adj.	well, hearty, hale

Aimless adj.	purposeful
Air vb.	hide, conceal
Airiness adj.	heaviness, sullenness, awkwardness
Airless adj.	breezy
Airy adj.	airless, heavy, sullen, awkward
Ajar adj.	shut
Alacrity n.	reluctance
Alarm n.	reassurance **vb.** reassure, soothe, comfort, calm
Alarming adj.	reassuring, calming, comforting, soothing
Alert adj.	listless, dulled, sluggish, lethargic, logy
Alertness n.	lethargy, listlessness
Alien n.	native **adj.**
Alienate vb.	conciliate
Alienation n.	conciliation
Alight vb.	board, embark, ascend **adj.**
Alike adj.	unlike
Alive adj.	dead, inactive, sluggish, moribund
All n.	nothing **adv.** partly
Allay vb.	arouse, worsen, intensify, aggravate
Allegation n.	denial
Allege vb.	deny
Allegiance n.	disloyalty, treachery
Allegorical adj.	literal
Alleviate vb.	intensify worsen

Allot vb.	withhold, retain
Allow vb.	forbid, prohibit, deny, withhold
Allowance n.	prohibition
Alloy vb.	separate, purify
All right adj.	unacceptable
Allure vb.	repel
Alluring adj.	repulsive
Ally n.	enemy, foe, adversary
Almost adv.	absolutely, completely
Alone adj.	accompanied, together
Aloof adj.	friendly, outgoing, cordial, warm
Alter vb.	keep, preserve, maintain
Alteration n.	preservation, maintenance, conservation
Altercation n.	agreement
Alternate vb.	fix
Altitude n.	depth
Altogether adv.	partially
Altruistic adj.	selfish
Always adv.	never, rarely
Amalgamate vb.	separate
Amalgamation n.	separation
Amass vb.	spend, disperse, dissipate, scatter
Amateur n.	professional, expert
Amaze vb.	bore, tire, disinterest
Amazing adj.	ordinary
Ambiguity n.	lucidity

Ambiguous

Ambiguous adj.	clear, unmistakable, certain
Ambitious adj.	lethargic, easy
Amble vb.	hurry
Ameliorate vb.	deteriorate
Amenable adj.	obstinate
Amend vb.	worsen, mar
Amenity n.	austerity
Amiable adj.	disagreeable, ill-tempered, cross, captious, touchy
Amicable adj.	hostile
Amiss adv.	properly, correctly, rightly **adj.** right, correct
Amity n.	hostility
Amnesty n.	condemnation
Amorous adj.	cold
Ample adj.	sacanty, insufficient, inadequate, cramped, confined
Amplify vb.	restrict, confine, narrow, abridge, reduce
Amuse vb.	bore, tire
Amusement n.	boredom, tedium
Amusing adj.	boring, tiring, tedious
Analogous adj.	different
Analogy n.	difference
Analysis n.	synthesis
Anarchaic adj.	ordered, organised
Anarchy n.	order
Ancestor n.	descendant

Ancestry n.	posterity
Anchor vb.	loosen, free, detach
Ancient adj.	new, fresh, recent, current, modern
Ancillery adj.	essential
Anfractuous adj.	straight
Angel n.	
Angelic adj.	diabolic
Anger n.	composure **vb.** appease
Angry adj.	happy, calm, content, tranquil
Anguish n.	joy, ecstasy, pleasure **vb.** soothe, comfort
Animate vb.	inanimate, dead, depress
Animated adj.	dull
Animosity n.	kindliness, love
Annex vb.	detach
Annexation n.	separation
Annihilate vb.	preserve
Annihilation n.	preservation
Announce vb.	suppress
Announcement n.	suppression
Annoy vb.	comfort, soothe, please
Annoyance n.	pleasure
Annul vb.	confirm
Answer n.	question, query, inquiry **vb.** ask, question, inquire
Antagonism n.	friendliness, geniality, cordiality, amity

Antagonist

Antagonist n.	ally, friend
Antagonistic adj.	friendly
Antidote n.	poison
Antipathy n.	sympathy
Antiquated adj.	modern, up-to-date, fashionable, instyle
Antique n.	modern, new, fresh, recent
Antisocial adj.	friendly
Anxiety n.	peacefulness, placidity, calmness, tranquility
Anxious adj.	peaceful, tranquil, calm
Apathetic adj.	enthusiastic
Apathy n.	enthusiasm
Apex n.	base
Apiece adj.	collectively
Apocryphal adj.	authentic
Apologetic adj.	unrepentant
Apostasy n.	loyalty
Apostate n.	loyal
Appal vb.	please, edify, reassure
Appaling adj.	wonderful
Apparent adj.	hidden, actual, real, evident
Apparently adv.	actually
Appeal n.	unattractiveness, **vb.** repel, repulse
Appear vb.	disappear, vanish, evaporate
Appearance n.	disappearance, vanishing
Appease vb.	aggravate, annoy

Append vb.	detach
Appendage adj.	essential
Applause n.	denunciation
Applaud vb.	disapprove, denounce, criticise, condemn
Applicable adj.	inapplicable, inappropriate
Apply vb.	neglect, ignore
Appoint vb.	dismiss, discharge, fire
Appointment n.	dismissal, discharge
Apportion vb.	retain
Appreciate vb.	scorn, depreciate, undervalue
Apprehend vb.	lose, release
Apprehension n.	self-assuredness, composure, confidence
Apprentice n.	master, professional
Approach vb.	recede n. exit
Approbation n.	censure
Appropriate adj.	inappropriate, unfit, inapt
Appropriation n.	return
Approval n.	disapproval, censure
Approve vb.	disapprove, deny, oppose
Approximate adj.	exact vb. differ
Approximately adv.	precisely
Apt adj.	unfit, unsuitable, ill-becoming, unlikely, slow, retarded, dense
Aptitude n.	incompetence

Aptness

Aptness n.	unsuitability, inappropriateness
Aquiline adj.	straight
Arbitrary adj.	reasoned
Archaic adj.	modern
Arched adj.	straight
Ardent adj.	cool
Ardour n.	apathy
Arduous adj.	easy
Area n.	whole
Argue vb.	agree, concur
Argument n.	agreement, accord, harmony
Arid adj.	fertile
Arise vb.	end, sink
Aristocrat n.	commoner, peasant
Arm vb.	disarm
Around prep.	amid
Arouse vb.	calm, pacify, settle, soothe
Arraign vb.	condone
Arrange vb.	disarrange, disturb, disorder
Array vb.	strip n. disorganisation, disarray, disorder
Arrest vb.	release, free, captivate, encourage, stimulate, bore
Arrival n.	departure, leaving
Arrive vb.	depart, leave
Arrogance n.	humility, humbleness, modesty
Arrogant adj.	humble, modest

Arrogate vb.	waive
Art n.	clumsiness, honesty
Artful adj.	artless, simple
Articulate vb.	sever **adj.** inarticulate, inexpressive
Artifice n.	honesty, incompetence
Artificial adj.	real, genuine, authentic, sincere
Artistic adj.	tasteless
Artless adj.	artful
Ascend vb.	descend
Ascendancy n.	servitude
Ascertain vb.	surmise
Ashamed adj.	proud
Asinine adj.	clever
Ask vb.	reply, answer
Askance adj.	straight
Askew adj.	straight
Asleep adj.	awake, alert
Asperity n.	mildness
Aspiration n.	apathy
Aspersion n.	condemnation
Assail vb.	resist, vindicate
Assailable adj.	unassailable
Assault n.	defence **vb.** defend
Assemble vb.	scatter, disperse, disassemble, dismantle
Assent vb.	refuse, dissent, deny **n.** refusal, denial

Assert vb.	deny, contradict, decline
Assertion n.	denial, contradiction
Assertive adj.	hesitant
Assets n.	liabilities
Asseverate vb.	deny
Asseveration n.	denial
Assiduity n.	indolence
Assiduous adj.	indolent
Assimilate vb.	reject
Assist vb.	hinder, obstruct, impede, thwart
Assistance n.	obstruction, interference
Associate vb.	disassociate, disconnect, disossiate
Association n.	dissociation
Assorted adj.	same, alike, homogeneous
Assuage vb.	aggravate, worsen
Assume vb.	know, discard
Assumed adj.	genuine
Assuming adj.	modest, humble
Assumption n.	knowledge, modesty
Assurance n.	equivocation, doubt
Assure vb.	equivocate, deny
Astonish vb.	bore, tire
Astonishing adj.	ordinary
Atheist n.	believer
Atone vb.	offend
Atonement n.	offence
Atrocious adj.	noble, excellent, kind

Atrocity n.	nobility, kindness
Atrophy vb.	flourish
Attach vb.	detach, unfasten, loosen, loose
Attachment n.	detachment, essential
Attack vb.	withdraw, retreat, praise, endors **n.** withdrawl, retreat
Attacker n.	defender
Attain vb.	fail, lose
Attainable adj.	impossible
Attainment n.	failure
Attempt vb.	achieve, accomplish **n.** achievement, accomplishment
Attend n.	inattention, absentmindedness, preoccupation, neglect
Attentive adj.	inattentive, preoccupied, absent-minded, neglectful
Attest vb.	deny
Attestation n.	denial
Attic n.	basement
Attract vb.	repel, repulse
Attraction n.	repulsion
Attractive adj.	unattractive, ugly, homely, plain
Attune vb.	disturb
Audacious adj.	timid, cowardly
Audacity n.	timidity
Audible adj.	inaudible
Augment vb.	decrease

B

Baby n.	adult **adj.**
Bacchanalian adj.	sober
Back n.	front **vb.** obstruct, advance
Back out adv.	onward **vb.** front
Backbite vb.	praise
Backbiting n.	praise
Backer n.	opponent
Backing n.	opposition
Backward adj.	advanced, forward, precocious **adv.** forward
Bad adj.	good, virtuous
Baffle vb.	enlighten, inform
Baleful adj.	beneficial, helpful, positive
Balloon vb.	shrink, shrivel
Balm n.	irritant
Balmy adj.	stormy, tempestuous, harsh
Ban vb.	permit, allow **n.** permission
Banal adj.	fresh, novel, original
Band n.	individual **vb.** separate
Bandy adj.	straight
Banish vb.	embrace, receive, admit, welcome
Bankrupt adj.	affluent
Bankruptcy n.	affluence

Bar n.	encouragement, aid **vb.** permit, allow
Barbarian adj.	civilised, cultured, cultivated, tasteful
Barbaric adj.	humane
Barbarity n.	humanity, refinement
Bare adj.	clothed, dressed, garbed **vb.** hide, conceal, disguise
Barefaced adj.	concealed
Barmy adj.	sensible
Barren adj.	fertile, fruitful, useful
Barricade vb.	release, free, open
Barrier n.	encouragement, aid, assistance
Base n.	top, peak, pinnacle
Base adj.	noble, exalted, virtuous, refined, valuable
Bashful adj.	self-assured, immodest, arrogant
Basis adj.	subordinate, subsidiary
Bass b.	treble
Bawdy adj.	decorous
Bawl vb.	whisper
Bear vb.	drop, resist, discard
Bearable adj.	unbearable
Bearish adj.	polite
Beastly adj.	humane
Beaten adj.	victorious, untrodden
Beautiful adj.	homely, unattractive, plain, ugly

Beautify

Beautify vb.	disfigure
Beauty n.	homliness, plainness, ugliness
Becoming adj.	unbecoming
Bedim vb.	illuminate
Bedlam n.	calm, quiet
Bedraggled adj.	neat
Befitting adj.	unsuitable
Before prep.	after **adv.** after-wards
Befriend vb.	oppose
Begin vb.	stop, end, finish, terminate
Beginner n.	professional, expert
Beginning n.	ending, finish, termination
Begrime vb.	cleanse
Behave vb.	misbehave, rebel
Behaviour n.	misbehaviour, rebelliousness
Behind prep.	before **adv.** ahead
Being n.	non-existense
Belated adj.	prompt
Belie vb.	confirm
Belief n.	disbelief
Believe vb.	doubt
Belittle vb.	build up, commend, flatter, extol
Belligerent adj.	peaceful
Bellow vb.	whisper
Beloved adj.	hated
Below prep.	above **adv.** above
Bemoan vb.	rejoice

Bend vb.	straighten
Beneath prep.	above **adv.** above
Benediction n.	curse
Benefaction n.	avarice
Beneficial adj.	unwholesome, disadvantageous
Benefit n.	disadvantage, loss **vb.** damage
Benevolent adj.	malevolent, mean, evil, cruel
Benign adj.	unfavourable, cold
Bent adj.	straight
Benumb vb.	stimulate
Berate vb.	commend
Bereave vb.	console, restore
Bereavement n.	consolation
Best adj.	worst
Bestow vb.	withhold, withdraw
Betray vb.	safeguard, protect, shelter
Better adj.	worse **vb.** worsen
Betterment n.	deterioration
Bewilder vb.	enlighten, clarify
Bewitch vb.	repel
Beyond prep.	within
Bias n.	impartiality, fairness
Bicker vb.	agree
Big adj.	small, insignificant, mean
Bigoted adj.	tolerant
Bind vb.	loosen, liberate, free, untie

Birth n.	death
Bit n.	lot
Bitter adj.	sweet, bland
Bizarre adj.	normal
Black adj.	white, light-skinned, clean, pure, pristine, bright, cheerful
Blame vb.	honour, credit
Blameless adj.	blameworthy
Blanch vb.	colour
Bland adj.	piquant
Blank adj.	filled, animated, alert
Blasé adj.	excited
Blasphemous adj.	reverent
Blasphemy n.	reverence
Blatant adj.	concealed, quiet
Blaze vb.	dwindle, die
Bleach vb.	darken, blacken
Bleak adj.	hopeful, cheerful, promising
Blend vb.	separate, divide
Bless vb.	curse
Blessing n.	curse
Blind adj.	sighted, seeing, knowing, clear-sighted, discerning, aware
Bliss n.	misery, unhappiness, torment
Blithe adj.	dejected
Bloat vb.	shrink

Block n.	passage, aid, advantage **vb.** aid, assist, forward, promote
Bloodless adj.	ruddy
Bloody adj.	gentle, kind
Bloom n.	decadence **vb.** wither, shrivel
Blossom vb.	wither, shrink, dwindle, fade
Blot vb.	clear
Blot out vb.	perpetuate
Blue adj.	happy, cheerful, optimistic
Bluff n.	shallow, gentle, sloping **adj.** subtle, indirect, reserved
Blunt adj.	sharp, keen, pointed diplomatic, tactful
Blur vb.	clarify, clear **n.** clarity
Blurred adj.	clear
Blush vb.	blanch **n.** pallor
Bluster n.	reticence
Blustery adj.	quiet
Board vb.	alight
Boastful adj.	modest
Bodily adj.	spiritual
Bogus adj.	genuine
Boisterous adj.	calm, quiet
Bold adj.	cowardly, fearful, timid, timorous, courteous, polite, deferential
Bond vb.	separate
Bondage n.	freedom
Boom n.	recession, decline **vb.** decline

Boon n.	drawback
Boorish adj.	cultivated, refined, well-mannered
Border n.	centre, middle
Bore vb.	interest, excite, arouse, captivate
Boredom n.	excitement
Boring adj.	exciting
Borrow vb.	lend
Boss n.	employee, worker, underling
Bossy adj.	meek
Botch vb.	accomplish **n.** success
Both adj. adv. conj.	Neither
Bother n.	comfort, solace **vb.** comfort
Bottom n.	top, topside
Bund adj.	unfettered, free
Boundless adj.	limited
Bountiful adj.	meagre, miserly
Bourgeois adj.	aristocratic, upper-class
Bow vb.	straighten, resists
Boy n.	man, girl
Bracing adj.	relaxing
Brag vb.	deprecate, depreciate **n.** modesty
Braid vb.	unravel
Brain(s) n.	stupidity
Brainy adj.	stupid
Brake vb.	accelerate
Branch vb.	converge

Brash adj.	cautious, modest
Bravado n.	modesty
Brave adj.	timid, cowardly, fearful, craven
Bravery n.	cowardice, timidity, fearfulness
Brazen adj.	modest, retiring, shy, self-effacing
Breach n.	observation, reconciliation
Breadth n.	length, narrowness
Break vb.	mend, repair, obey
Break up vb. phr.	unite
Break down vb. phr.	restroration
Breeze n.	calm
Brevity n.	prolixity
Bridge vb.	divide
Bridle vb.	loose, free, release
Brief adj.	long, extended, protracted, extensive, comprehensive, exhaustive
Bright adj.	dull, dim, lusterless, boring, dull, colorless, stupid, slow, backward
Brilliant adj.	dull, lusterless, mediocore, second-rate
Brim n.	centre, middle
Bring vb.	withdraw, remove
Brink n.	center
Brisk adj.	slow, sluggish, lethargic, heavy, still, oppressive
Brittle adj.	flexible, supple, elastic

Broach vb.	seal
Broad adj.	narrow, constricted, limited, negligible
Broaden vb.	restrict
Broad-minded adj.	narrow-minded, prejudiced, bigoted, petty
Broke adj.	rich
Broken adj.	mended, continuous, fluent
Brother n.	sister
Brusque adj.	courteous, polite, personable

C

Cacophonous adj.	harmonious
Cadaverous adj.	ruddy
Cagey adj.	guileless, innocent, naive, straightforward
Calamitous adj.	fortunate
Calamity n.	boon, blessing
Calculate vb.	guess, assume
Calculating adj.	ingenuous, simple, direct, guileless
Calculation n.	assumption, guess
Callous adj.	tender
Callow adj.	experienced
Calm adj.	tempestuous, disturbed, excited **n.** turmoil, upheaval, disturbance **vb.** upset, excite, disturb

Calmness n.	disturbances, agitation
Camaraderie n.	enmity
Camouflage vb.	expose
Cancel vb.	ratify, confim
Cancellation n.	confirmation
Canker vb.	purify
Cantankerous adj.	affable, friendly
Capability n.	incapability
Capable adj.	inept, incompetent, unskilled
Capacious adj.	narrow
Capacitate vb.	prevent
Capacity n.	incapacity, inability
Capital adj.	trivial, minor, unimportant, secondary
Capitulate vb.	resist
Capricious adj.	steady, reliable, firm
Captious adj.	appreciative, affable
Captivate vb.	repel
Captivation adj.	repulsive
Captivity n.	freedom, liberty
Capture vb.	release, free, liberate
Cardinal adj.	secondary, subordinate, auxiliary
Care n.	indifference, unconcern, carelessness
Carefree adj.	anxious, concern
Careful adj.	incautious, heedless, careless, messy, cautions, prudent, painstaking

38 Carelessness

Carelessness n.	care
Carnal n.	chaste, spiritual
Carp n.	praise
Carping adj.	appreciative
Carry vb.	drop, deter
Carry on vb.	stop
Cast vb.	keep, retain
Casual adj.	planned, calculated, deliberate, premeditated, formal, dressy
Catastrophe n.	boon, blessing, triumph
Catch vb.	release, free, drop
Catching adj.	repulsive
Categorical adj.	vague
Cause n.	effect
Caustic adj.	mild
Caution n.	heedlessness, carelessness, incaution, rashness
Cautious adj.	rash, heedless, headstrong, foolish, indiscreet
Cease vb.	being, start
Cede vb.	retain
Celebrate vb.	ignore, disregard
Celebrate adj.	anonymous, unknown
Celestial adj.	earthly
Censure n.	approval, praise vb. praise, approval, applaud
Center n.	edge, brim

Central adj.	secondary, auxiliary, side, incidental, extreme, peripheral
Centralise vb.	decentralise
Ceremonial adj.	casual
Ceremonious adj.	unceremonious, informal
Certain adj.	doubtful, uncertain, questionable, unlikely
Certainly adv.	doubtfully, dubiously, questionably
Certainly n.	doubt, uncertainly
Certify vb.	deny
Cessation n.	continuance
Chafe vb.	soothe, appease
Chagrin n.	pleasure **vb.** please
Chain vb.	loose
Chance n.	certainty, inevitability **adj.** intentional
Change vb.	endure, remain, endurance, steadfastness, immutability, conservation
Chaos n.	tranquility, order, organization, tidiness
Chaostic adj.	ordered, organized, neat, systematic
Characteristic adj.	general
Charge vb.	retreat, flee, absolve, excuse, pardon
Charitable adj.	mean, petty, stingy, narrow-minded
Charm vb.	repel **n.** repulsion
Charming adj.	repulsive

Chaste

Chaste adj.	impure, worldly, sinful, immodest
Chasten vb.	pamper
Chastise vb.	reward
Chastity n.	corruption
Cheap adj.	costly, expensive, dear, elegant, well-made
Check vb.	advance, continue, foster, promote, encourage
Cheer n.	discouragement, derision **vb.** discourage, sadden, boo, hiss
Cheerful adj.	sad, gloomy, morose, downhearted, dejected
Cheerfulness n.	dejection
Cherish vb.	scorn, undervalue, deprecate, disparage, abandon
Chicanery n.	honesty
Chide vb.	praise, extol, commend
Chiefly adv.	lastly, last
Child n.	adult
Childish adj.	adult, grownup, mature, seasoned
Chill n.	warmth, heat **adj.** warm, heated, hot
Chilly adj.	warm, friendly
Chivalrous adj.	rude, impolite, crude, uncivil, cowardly
Choose vb.	reject
Chronic adj.	acute, fleeting, temporary
Chubby adj.	lean
Churlish adj.	polite, generous

Circulation adj.	direct
Circular adj.	straight, square
Circulate vb.	retain, stagnate
Circumference n.	diameter
Circumvent vb.	confront
Circumvention n.	honesty
Civil adj.	impolite, rude, crude, churlish
Claim vb.	waive
Clammy adj.	dry
Clamor n.	quiet, serenity, tranquility
Clamorous adj.	quiet, tranquil, peaceful
Clandestine adj.	open
Clarification n.	mystification
Clarify vb.	confuse, muddle, obscure
Clash n.	harmony, agreement, accord **vb.** harmonize, blend, agree, match
Clasp vb.	release, detach
Classification n.	muddle
Clean adj.	dirty, spoiled, impure, contaminated **vb.** soil, dirty, pollute
Cleanse vb.	pollute
Clear adj.	confused, muddled, overcast, cloudy, dark, dubious, questionable, obstructed, blocked, blockaded **vb.** fill, clutter, implicate, involve, obstruct, block, blockade

Clearly adv.	dubiously, questionably
Cleave vb.	unite
Clench vb.	relax
Clever adj.	stupid, slow, backward, dull, clumsy, maladroit, inept
Climb vb.	descend
Clinch vb.	loose
Cling vb.	separate
Clip vb.	detach, elongate
Clock vb.	reveal, show, display, expose
Clog vb.	free
Cloistered adj.	sociable
Close vb.	open, unlock, begin, start **adj.** far, distant, fresh, clear, generous, open-handed, charitable
Clothe vb.	strip, undress
Cloudy adj.	clearheaded, lucid, clarified, sunny, clear, brilliant, cloudless
Club vb.	separate
Clump vb.	disperse, scatter
Clumsy adj.	graceful, adroit, skilful, polished, dexterous
Cluster vb.	disperse, scatter
Coalition n.	separation
Coarse adj.	fine, refined, cultivated, genteel, suave
Coax vb.	coerce, bully, force
Cogent adj.	weak

Cognate adj.	unrelated
Cognisance n.	ignorance
Coherent adj.	incoherent, illogical
Cohesion n.	disintegration
Coincidence n.	plan, scheme, plot, prearrangement
Coincidental adj.	planned
Cold adj.	hot, warm, temperate, friendly, warm, compassionate, outgoing
Collaborate vb.	compete
Collect vb.	disperse, scatter, dispel
Collection n.	dispersion
Collision n.	accord
Colloquial adj.	formal
Collusive adj.	honest
Colourful adj.	dull, flat, uninteresting
Coltish adj.	lethargic
Colossal adj.	tiny, miniature, microscopic, minuscule
Combat vb.	surrender, yield, succumb
Combination n.	separation, division
Combine vb.	separate, divide
Come vb.	go, leave, depart
Come vb.	go, leave, depart
Comely adj.	ugly, plain
Comfort vb.	upset, agitate, disturb, discompose, uncertainty, discomfort

Comfortable adj.	uncomfortable, strained, tense, edgy
Comparative adj.	absolute
Comparison n.	contrast
Compassionate adj.	unsympathetic, coldhearted, harsh
Compatible adj.	incompatible, disagreeable, at odds
Compel vb.	coax, wheedle, cajole
Compelling adj.	boring
Compendious adj.	extended
Compete vb.	accord, reconcile
Competence n.	incompetence, ineptitude
Competent adj.	incompetent, inept, awkward, gauche
Competitor n.	friend, ally, colleague
Complement vb.	conflict, clash
Complementary adj.	conflicting
Complete adj.	unfinished, incomplete, partial **vb.** begin, start, commence
Complex adj.	simple, basic, plain, uncomplicated, rudimentary
Compliment n.	insult, aspersion, affront **vb.** insult, affront, disparage
Comply vb.	refuse
Component n.	whole

Comport vb.	differ
Conciliation n.	estrangement
Concise adj.	lengthy
Conclude vb.	begin, commence, start
Conclusion n.	beginning, start, opening, commencement
Conclusive adj.	inconclusive
Concord n.	discord
Concrete adj.	vague, undetermined, abstract, general
Concur vb.	dissent
Concurrence n.	disagreement
Concurrent adj.	divergent, discordant
Condemn vb.	praise, loud, extol, applaud, pardon, absolve, excuse, acquit
Condemnation n.	acquittal, praise
Condemnatory adj.	laudatory
Condense vb.	expand, enlarge, swell, increase
Condescending adj.	humble
Conditional adj.	absolute
Condole vb.	rejoice
Condone vb.	punish
Conduce vb.	hinder
Confederate vb.	separate
Confer vb.	withdraw, retrieve

Confess

Confess vb.	deny
Confession n.	denial
Confidence n.	distrust, mistrust, doubt, shyness, modesty, diffidence
Confident adj.	timid, uncertain, shy, self-effacing
Confindentail adj.	public
Confidentially adv.	publicly
Confine vb.	release, free
Confinement n.	liberation, freedom
Confirm vb.	deny, disclaim, disavow, refute
Confirmed adj.	infrequent, occasional
Confiscate vb.	restore
Conflict vb.	agree, harmonize, concur, coincide **n.** agreement, harmony, concurrence
Confluence n.	divergence
Conform vb.	rebel, disagree, vary
Confront vb.	evade
Confuse vb.	enlighten, edify, illuminate, clarify, differentiate, distinguish
Confusion n.	enlightenment, understanding, comprehension, organization, tidiness
Confute vb.	prove
Conglomerate vb.	disperse
Congregate vb.	disperse, scatter, dissipate, dispel

Congruous adj.	incongruous
Conjectural adj.	proven
Conjecture n.	proof
Conjoin vb.	sever
Conjunction n.	disconnection, separation, diversion
Connect vb.	disconnect, disjoin, sever, dissociate, disassociate
Connected adj.	unconnected, disconnected
Connection n.	dissociation, disassociation
Conquer vb.	surrender, yield
Conquest n.	failure, surrender
Conscientious adj.	irresponsible, careless, slovenly
Conscious adj.	unaware, insensitive, asleep, insensible, comatose, careless, indifferent, slack, negligent
Consecrate vb.	desecrate
Consecutive adj.	discontinuous
Consent vb.	refuse, dissent **n.** refusal, dissent
Consequence n.	cause, impetus
Consequential adj.	unimportant, trivial, minor, insignificant
Conservative adj.	liberal, radical, reckless, rash, adventurous, foolhardy
Conserve vb.	squander, waste, use
Consider vb.	ignore, disregard, disdain
Construct vb.	destroy, demolish, raze

Construction n.	demolition
Constructive adj.	destructive, ruinous
Consult vb.	ignore
Consume vb.	conserve
Consumer n.	producer
Consummate vb.	abort
Consumption n.	conservation
Contact n.	isolation
Contain vb.	release
Contaminate vb.	cleanse
Contamination n.	purification, cleaning
Contemplate vb.	ignore
Contemplative adj.	indifferent, inattentive, thoughtless
Contemporary adj.	antecedent, succeeding
Contempt n.	admiration, approbation
Contemptible adj.	admirable, honorable
Contemptuous adj.	humble, modest, self-effacing
Content adj.	dissatisfied, restless, discontented
Contention n.	agreement

Continual adj.	irregular, intermittent, occasional
Continually adv.	occasionally
Continuation n.	cessation
Continue vb.	stop, interrupt, discontinue, cease
Continuous adj.	irregular, intermittent, sporadic, broken
Contort vb.	straighten
Contraband adj.	lawful
Contract vb.	expand, swell, enlarge
Contradict vb.	confirm
Contradiction n.	agreement, harmony
Contrary adj.	similar, like, complementary, obliging, agreeable, tractable
Contrast n.	similarity, agreement, likeness
Contravene vb.	keep, assist
Contribute vb.	withhold, deny
Contrite adj.	unrepentant
Controversial adj.	indisputable
Controversy n.	agreement, harmony, accord
Convenience n.	inconvenience, hindrance
Convenient adj.	inconvenient, awkward
Conventional adj.	unusual, extraordinary, exotic, bizarre
Converge vb.	diverge

Conversant adj.	unfamiliar
Converse adj.	same
Convict vb.	acquit
Conviction n.	doubt
Convincing adj.	unconvincing
Convivial adj.	stern, solemn, unsociable, gloomy
Convulse vb.	compose
Cool adj.	warm, hot, heated, excited, overwrought, hysterical, friendly, warm, outgoing **vb.** warm, heat, excite, agitate
Coop vb.	liberate
Cooperate vb.	oppose
Cooperative adj.	rebellious, individual
Copious adj.	scanty, meagre, paltry, scarce
Copy n.	original
Cordial adj.	distant, unfriendly, ill-tempered, hostile
Core n.	outside, exterior, surface
Corporal adj.	mental
Corporeal adj.	spiritual
Corpulence n.	thinness
Correct adj.	incorrect, wrong, inexact, erroneous
Corrective adj.	detrimental
Correctness n.	incorrectness, impropriety
Correlation n.	independence

Correspond vb.	diverge, differ, vary
Corrigible adj.	intractable
Corroborate vb.	invalidate
Corrode vb.	restore
Corrugate vb.	smooth
Corrupt adj.	honest, upright, scrupulous, pure, sanctified **vb.** purify, edify, sanctify
Cosset vb.	neglect
Costly adj.	Inexpensive, low-cost, cheap
Countenance vb.	prohibit, forbid, oppose **n.** disapproval
Counter adj.	like
Countract vb.	assist
Counterfeit adj.	genuine, real, authentic
Country n.	city
Couple vb.	separate
Courage n.	cowardice, fearfulness, weakness
Courageous adj.	cowardly, timid, fearful
Courteous adj.	rude, impolite, discourteous
Courtesy n.	rudeness, discourtesy
Cover vb.	uncover, expose, reveal
Covert adj.	open
Covetous adj.	generous
Coward n.	hero
Cowardice n.	bravery
Cowardly adj.	brave
Cower vb.	confront

Coy adj.	bold, brash, forward
Crack vb.	mend, resist
Cracked adj.	guileless, gullible, open, naive
Craggy adj.	smooth
Crank adj.	good-natured, cheerful, happy
Crapulent adj.	sober
Crave vb.	renounce, relinquish, spurn
Craven adj.	brave **n.** hero
Crawl vb.	race
Crazy adj.	same, rational, lucid
Create vb.	destroy, abolish
Creation n.	destruction
Creative adj.	unimaginative
Credence n.	disbelief
Credible adj.	incredible, unbelievable, inconceivable
Credit n.	discredit, blame **vb.** discredit
Creditable adj.	discreditable, dishonorable, shameful
Credulous adj.	suspicious
Crestfallen adj.	elated
Criminal adj.	lawful
Crinkle vb.	smooth
Critical adj.	unimportant, trivial
Criticism n.	praise
Criticize vb.	praise
Curt adj.	polite, friendly, pleasant
Curtail vb.	lengthen, extend

Curve vb.	straighten
Customary adj.	unusual, rare, unaccustomed
Cut vb.	join, extend, acknowledge
Cutting adj.	soothing

D

Daft adj.	sensible
Dainty adj.	clumsy, lumpish, oafish
Dalliance n.	haste
Dally vb.	hurry
Damage n.	repair, rebuild, improve, fix, reparation
Damnation n.	blessing
Damp adj.	dry, arid
Dampen vb.	dry, encourage
Dandy n.	slob **adj.** awful
Danger n.	safety, security
Dangerous adj.	safe, secure
Dank adj.	dry
Dare vb.	quail
Daring n.	timidity, cowardice
Dark adj.	light, illuminated, bright, cheerful, happy
Darken vb.	lighten, illuminated, bright, cheerful, happy

Dart

Dart vb.	amble
Dastardly adj.	brave, noble
Dated adj.	modern, lasted
Daunt vb.	encourage, enspirit
Dauntless adj.	timid, cowardly, fearful
Dawdle vb.	hurry
Dawn n.	sunset, dusk, nightfall, end, finish, conclusion
Daybreak n.	nightfall
Dazzle vb.	bore
Dead adj.	alive, animate, active, functioning
Deaf adj.	conscious, aware
Deafening adj.	quiet
Dear adj.	hateful, loathsome, cheap, inexpensive, reasonable
Dearth n.	abundance
Death n.	life, birth
Debar vb.	admit
Debase vb.	raise, purify
Debatable adj.	certain
Debate n.	agreement, accord vb. agree, decide
Debauch vb.	purify
Debilitate vb.	strengthen
Debility n.	strength
Debt n.	asset
Decadence n.	rise
Decay vb.	grow, progress, flourish, growth

Deceased adj.	alive
Deceit n.	honesty, forthrightness, openness
Deceitful adj.	honest, sincere
Decency n.	impropriety
Decent adj.	indecent, improper, indecorous, unsuitable
Deception n.	honesty, openness, frankness, probity
Deceptive adj.	real, true, authentic
Decide vb.	hesitate, waver
Decipher vb.	encode
Decision n.	indecision
Decisive adj.	indecisive, inconclusive
Declaration n.	denial, suppression
Declare vb.	deny, suppress
Decline vb.	agree, accept, improve, increase, grow **n.** improvement, ascent
Decomposition n.	synthesis
Decorate vb.	deface, mar
Decorous adj.	unseemly
Decorum n.	impropriety
Decrease vb.	increase, expand **n.** increase, expansion
Decrement n.	increment
Definite adj.	indefinite, undetermined, vague
Deflate vb.	inflate, boost
Deft adj.	inept, maladroit, clumsy, awkward

Defunct adj.	living
Defy vb.	yield, submit, surrender, obey
Degrade vb.	exalt, promote
Dehydrate vb.	moisten
Dejected adj.	happy, cheerful, optimistic
Delay vb.	hasten, forward, advance
Delectable adj.	repulsive
Delete vb.	insert, add
Deleterious adj.	healthy, healthful, constructive, helpful, beneficial
Deliberate adj.	accidental, unintentional, unplanned
Delicate adj.	clumsy, heavy-handed, coarse, hale, hearty, strong
Delicious adj.	unpleasant, unpalatable
Delight n.	revulsion, disgust, displeasure vb. displease, revolt, disgust
Delightful adj.	disagreeable, unpleasant, nasty
Delirious adj.	sane
Delirium n.	sanity
Deliver vb.	confine, imprison, enslave
Deliverance n.	capture
Deluge n.	drought
Delusion n.	reality
Demand vb.	relinquish, waive
Demean vb.	exalt
Demise n.	birth
Democratic adj.	autocratic

Demolish vb.	build, construct, erect
Demolition n.	construction, erection
Demon n.	angel
Demonic adj.	angelic
Demonstrative adj.	reserved
Demoralize vb.	encourage
Demote vb.	promote
Demur vb.	consent
Denial n.	confirmation, consent
Denigrate vb.	praise
Denounce vb.	extol
Dense adj.	scarce, scanty, clever
Denude vb.	admit, concede, confess, allow, permit
Depart vb.	arrive, come
Departure n.	arrival
Dependable adj.	unreliable
Dependence n.	independent
Deplete vb.	fill
Deplorable adj.	commendable
Depose vb.	enthrone
Deposit vb.	withdraw **n.** withdrawal
Deposition n.	enthronement
Deprave vb.	improve
Depraved adj.	virtuous
Depravity n.	virtuous

Depravity

Depravity n.	virtue
Deprecate vb.	praise, applaud, commend
Depress vb.	cheer, exhilarate, exalt
Depressed adj.	elated
Depression n.	elevation, eminence, elation, happiness, boom
Deprivation n.	endowment
Deprive vb.	supply, provide, provision
Depth n.	shallowness, surface, height, tallness, loftiness
Depute vb.	dismiss
Derangement n.	sanity
Dereliction n.	observance
Deride vb.	respect
Derisive adj.	respectful
Derogate vb.	extol
Derogatory adj.	flattering
Descend vb.	ascend, climb, embark
Descendant n.	ancestors
Desecrate vb.	consecrate
Desert adj.	fertile
Desert vb.	join, accompany
Deserter n.	loyalist
Deserted adj.	populous
Desiccate vb.	moisten
Desirable adj.	undesirable, unattractive, repellent
Desire vb.	loathe, abhor, detest

Desist vb.	persist, continue
Desolate adj.	crowded, populous, teeming, cheerful, happy
Despair n.	joy, hope, optimism
Desperate adj.	calm, collected
Despicable adj.	admirable, honorable, worthy
Despise vb.	admire, like, honour
Despondency n.	hopefulness, cheerfulness
Despotic adj.	democratic
Destitute adj.	wealthy, rich
Destroy vb.	create, start, undertake
Destruction n.	creation, beginning
Desultory adj.	methodical
Detach vb.	attach, connect, hitch
Detached adj.	attached, involved
Detail vb.	summarise
Detailed adj.	cursory
Detain vb.	forward, hurry, rush, free
Detention n.	release
Deter vb.	encourage
Deteriorate vb.	improve
Determination n.	irresolution
Determine vb.	waver, hesitate
Detest vb.	like, love, appreciate, savor
Detestable adj.	adorable, lovable
Dethrone vb.	enthrone

Detract vb.	enhance
Detraction n.	flattery
Detriment n.	benefit
Detrimental adj.	Beneficial
Develop vb.	deteriorate, degenerate
Devilish adj.	angelic
Devoid adj.	full
Devote vb.	relinquish, withdraw, withhold, ignore
Devoted adj.	indifferent
Devout adj.	indifferent, scornful
Dexterous adj.	clumsy, awkward
Diabolic adj.	angelic
Diaphanous adj.	opaque
Dictatorial adj.	democratic
Die vb.	live, flourish, grow
Differ vb.	coincide, agree
Difference n.	similarity, likeness, kinship, compatibility
Different adj.	similar, alike, identical
Difficult adj.	easy, simple
Difficulty adj.	ease
Diffident adj.	confident, brash, forward
Diffuse adj.	concentrated, concise **vb.** gather
Diffusion n.	agglomeration
Dignify vb.	humiliate, degrade, shame
Dilapidated adj.	restored

Dilapidation n.	renovation, restoration
Dilate vb.	contract, abridge
Dilatory adj.	prompt
Dim adj.	bright, brilliant, clear **vb.** brighten, illuminate
Diminish vb.	enlarge, increase, wax
Diminution n.	increase
Diminutive adj.	large, big, great, huge, gigantic
Din n.	silence
Dingy adj.	bright, cheerful
Dip vb.	rise
Diplomacy n.	tactlessness
Diplomatic adj.	tactless
Dire adj.	delightful, wonderful, pleasant, splendid
Direct adj.	crooked, indirect, swerving, equivocal, circuitous, dishonest, untruthful **vb.** mislead
Dirt n.	cleanness, cleanliness
Dirty adj.	clean, cleanse, purify
Disability n.	fitness
Disable vb.	strengthen
Disadvantage n.	benefit, advantage, convenience
Disagree vb.	agree, coincide
Disagreeable adj.	agreeable, pleasant
Disallow vb.	sanction, accept
Disappear vb.	appear, emerge

Disappoint vb.	satisfy, please, gratify
Disappointment n.	satisfaction, pleasure, gratification
Disapprove vb.	approve, sanction
Disarm vb.	arm
Disarray vb.	arm
Disarray vb.	order
Disbelief n.	credulity, certainty, belief
Disburden vb.	encumber
Disburse vb.	save
Discard vb.	retain
Discern vb.	miss
Discernible adj.	imperceptible
Discernment n.	stupidity, dullness
Discharge vb.	employ, hire, enlist, appoint n. enlistment, appointment, detention
Disciple n.	leader, guide
Discipline n.	indiscipline, indulgence, carelessness, negligence, sloppiness, messiness
Disclaim vb.	confess
Disclaimer n.	confession
Disclose vb.	hide, disguise, mask, conceal
Disgust n.	liking, admiration
Disgusting adj.	attractive, appealing
Dishearten vb.	encourage
Disheveled adj.	tidy
Dishonest adj.	honest, straightforward, upright

Display 63

Dishonor vb.	honour **n.** esteem
Disinclined adj.	willing
Disinfect vb.	contaminate
Disinter vb.	bury
Disjoined adj.	coherent
Dislike vb.	like **n.** liking
Dislodge vb.	place
Dismal adj.	cheerful, happy, charming, lighthearted
Dismantle vb.	assemble
Dismay vb.	hearten, encourage, reassure
Dismiss vb.	retain, engage, hire, employ
Disorder n.	order, neatness, organization
Disown vb.	acknowledge
Disparage vb.	extol
Disparate adj.	identical
Disparity n.	equality
Dispatch vb.	retain **n.** slowness, reluctance, hesitancy
Dispel vb.	collect
Dispensable adj.	essential
Dispense vb.	withhold
Disperse vb.	gather, collect, assemble
Dispirit vb.	encourage
Dispirited adj.	happy, cheerful, optimistic
Displace vb.	fix, retain
Display vb.	disguise, hide, conceal, cover

Displease vb.	please, appease
Dispossess vb.	house
Disproportion adj.	equality
Disprove vb.	prove
Dispute vb.	agree, concur **n.** agreement, accord, concurrence
Disregard vb.	heed, acknowledge
Disrespectful adj.	respectful, polite, courteous
Disrobe vb.	dress
Disseminate vb.	suppress
Dissent n.	assent, approval
Dissenter n.	conformist
Dissever vb.	unite
Dissipate vb.	hoard, collect
Dissociate vb.	join
Dissolve vb.	solidify, endure, unite
Dissonance n.	harmony, accord
Dissuade vb.	urge, persuade
Distant adj.	near, close
Distasteful adj.	pleasant
Distend vb.	contract
Distinct adj.	indistinct, vague, uncertain, obscure
Distinction n.	insignificance
Distinguish vb.	blend, join, confuse
Distinguished adj.	obscure, unknown, undistinguished

Distort vb.	straighten
Distract vb.	concentrate, focus
Distracted adj.	composed, concentrated
Distraught adj.	calm
Distress n.	happiness, tranquility, peacefulness **vb.** please, charm, satisty
Distribute vb.	collect, gather, assemble
Distrust vb.	trust **n.** trust, confidence
Disturb vb.	calm, pacify, arrange
Disturbance n.	serenity, calm, tranquility, peace
Disturbed adj.	normal
Dither vb.	decide
Diverge vb.	join, converge, merge
Diverse n.	similar
Diversion n.	routine
Diversity n.	similarity, likeness
Divert vb.	clothe
Down adv. up **adj.**	cheerful
Downcast adj.	cheerful, happy, lighthearted, encourage
Downfall n.	rise
Downgrade vb.	upgrade, improve, appreciate
Downhearted adj.	cheerful, happy, enthusiastic
Downward adv.	upward
Drab adj.	bright
Drag vb.	push, hurry

Draggle vb.	hurry
Drain vb.	fill, fulfill
Drape vb.	divest
Drastic adj.	moderate
Draw vb.	push, propel, repel
Drawback n.	advantage
Dream n.	reality
Dreary adj.	cheerful, hopeful, bright, encouraging, exciting
Drench vb.	dry
Dress vb.	undress, disrobe, strip
Drive vb.	deter n. apathy
Droll adj.	serious
Droop vb.	straighten, rise, flourish
Drop vb.	rise, continue
Drought n.	deluge, glut

E

Eager adj.	indifferent, uninterested, uninvolved
Eagerness n.	indifference
Early adj.	late, latest adv. late
Earn vb.	forfeit, pay
Earnest adj.	insincere, frivolous, indifferent, casual, flippant
Earnings n.	payments, expenses, expenditures
Earthly adj.	heavenly, spiritual

Earthy adj.	refined, elegant, tasteful
Ease n.	difficulty, trouble, effort vb. aggravate, heighten, worsen, intensity
Easy adj.	difficult, uneasy, strenuous, awkward
Ebb vb.	advance, flood, grow n. high tide, flood tide
Ebullient adj.	lethargic, gloomy, sad, depressed
Eccentric adj.	normal
Economical adj.	wasteful, lavish, unsparing, extravagant
Economize vb.	squander
Ecstasy n.	misery, unhappiness, agony
Ecstatic adj.	miserable, sad
Edge n.	middle, center
Edgy adj.	undisturbed, tranquil, peaceful bland, placid
Edible adj.	inedible
Edification n.	corruption
Educated adj.	ignorant
Elect vb.	reject
Elegant adj.	crude, unpolished, coarse, tasteless
Element n.	whole
Elevated adj.	low, base
Elevation n.	depth, lowering
Eligible adj.	ineligible
Eliminate vb.	include

Elite n.	dregs (of society), proletariat, mob
Elongate vb.	condense
Eloquent adj.	inarticulate, inexpressive, tongue-tied
Elucidate vb.	mystify
Elude vb.	include, add, face, confront
Emaciated adj.	obese
Emanate vb.	culminate, absorb
Emancipate vb.	enslave
Emasculate vb.	strengthen
Embalm vb.	forget
Embargo n.	license
Embark vb.	disembark
Embellish vb.	disfigure, mar
Embolden vb.	discourage
Embowed vb.	straight
Embrace vb.	exclude, bar, reject
Embroil vb.	extricate
Embryonic adj.	mature
Emerge vb.	recede, retreat, disappear
Emigrate vb.	immigrate
Eminence n.	obscurity
Eminent adj.	unknown, undistinguished, ordinary, commonplace
Emotional adj.	calm, tranquil, placid
Emphasis n.	understate
Emphatic adj.	quiet, lax, unforceful
Employ vb.	waste, ignore, disregard, dismiss

Employee n.	employed, boss
Employer n.	employee, worker
Empty adj.	full, filled vb. fill
Empyrean adj.	earthly
Enable vb.	prevent
Enact vb.	abrogate
Enamour vb.	repel
Enchain vb.	loose
Enchant vb.	bore, tire, repel
Enchanting adj.	repulsive
Enclose vb.	exclude
Encompass vb.	exclude
Encounter vb.	avoid
Encourage vb.	discourage, deter, dissuade
End n.	beginning, start, opening, launch vb. begin, start, launch, initiate
Endanger vb.	protect, secure
Endemic adj.	universal
Endow vb.	divest
Endure vb.	fail, perish, die
Enemy n.	friend, colleague, cohort, ally
Energetic adj.	lazy, indolent, sluggish, lax, lethargic
Energise vb.	enervate
Energy n.	lethargy, feebleness
Enervate vb.	invigorate, energise
Enfeeble vb.	strengthen
Enforce vb.	waive

Engage vb.	disengage, fire, dismiss, discharge
Engaging adj.	boring, ordinary, repulsive
Engorge vb.	erase
Engross vb.	bore
Enhance vb.	depreciate
Enigma n.	solution
Enjoyment n.	displeasure, abhorrence
Enkindle vb.	extinguish
Enlarge vb.	decrease, diminish, wane, shrink
Enlargement n.	contraction
Enlighten vb.	confuse
Enlightened adj.	ignorant
Enlist vb.	leave, abandon, quit
Enmesh vb.	extricate
Enmity n.	friendship
Ennoble vb.	degrade
Enormous adj.	small, diminutive, tiny, slight, infinitesimal
Enough adj.	insufficient
Enrage vb.	soothe, appease, calm, pacify
Enrapture vb.	repel
Enrich vb.	impoverish, disfigure
Enroll vb.	leave, quit, abandon
Ensemble n.	element adv. individually
Enslave vb.	liberate, release
Ensue vb.	precede
Ensure vb.	imperil

Entangle vb.	extricate
Enter vb.	leave
Enterprising adj.	indolent, lazy, unresourceful, sluggish
Entertain vb.	bore, tire
Enthrall vb.	bore
Enthusiasm n.	indifference, unconcern, apathy
Enthusiastic adj.	aloof, indifferent, unconcerned, apathetic
Entice vb.	deter
Entire adj.	partial, incomplete, ferent, unconcerned, apathetic
Entice vb.	deter
Entire adj.	partial, incomplete, separated, divided
Entirely adv.	partially
Entitle vb.	disqualify
Entrance n.	exit
Entrance vb.	repel
Entrap vb.	loose
Entreat vb.	command
Entreaty n.	order
Entrench vb.	move
Entwine vb.	separate, extricate
Enunciate vb.	stammer, suppress
Convey n.	contentedness, generosity
Ephemeral adj.	permanent
Epitomise vb.	amplify

Equal adj.	unequal, different, uneven, regular
Equality n.	inequality
Equanimity n.	agitation
Equip vb.	divest
Equivalence n.	difference
equivocal adj.	clear
Eradicate vb.	restore
Erase vb.	engrave, include, add
Evaporate vb.	appear, condense
Evasive adj.	straightforward
Even adj.	bumpy, irregular, unequal, unbalanced, divergent
Evening n.	dawn, sunrise
Event n.	cause
Even-tempered adj.	hot-tempered, hot-headed
Eventful adj.	uneventful
Eventuate vb.	begin
Eventual adj.	current, present
Ever adv.	never
Everlasting adj.	brief, passing, temporary, transient
Every adj.	none
Everyday adj.	rare, unusual
Evict vb.	house
Evident adj.	unclear, obscure, doubtful, uncertain
Evil adj.	virtuous, moral, upright, good, beneficial, advantageous, useful n. goodness, virtue, uprightness

Evince vb.	conceal
Evoke vb.	stifle
Evolution n.	retrogression
Exacerbate vb.	soothe, appease
Exact adj.	inexact, inaccurate, faulty
Exaggerate vb.	minimize, understate, diminish
Exhibit vb.	conceal, hide, disguise
Exhilarate vb.	depress
Exhort vb.	deter, discourage
Exiguous adj.	ample
Exit n.	entrance, arrival vb. enter
Exodus n.	arrival
Exonerate vb.	charge, compel
Exorbitant adj.	reasonable, normal, moderate
Exotic adj.	native, ordinary
Expand vb.	shrink, shrivel, contract
Expansive adj.	narrow, reserved
Expatiate vb.	summarize
Expedient adj.	unwise
Expedite vb.	delay
Expeditious adj.	slow
Expel vb.	invite, accept
Expend vb.	conserve, reserve, ration, save
Expenditure n.	income
Expensive adj.	inexpensive, modest, low-priced, low-cost, cheap
Experience n.	inexperience, naivete

Experienced adj.	inexperienced, untutored, naïve, unpracticed
Expert adj.	unskilled, untrained, inexperienced, novice
Expire vb.	begin
Explain vb.	mystify
Expletive adj.	essential
Explicit adj.	implied
Expose vb.	conceal, hide, cover, mask, protect
Express adj.	slow, local vb. suppress
Expulsion n.	welcome
Exquisite adj.	ugly, ordinary
Extend vb.	contract, shorten, abbreviate, curtail, withhold
Extensive adj.	confined, restricted, narrow, limited
Extenuate vb.	exaggerate
Exterior n.	interior, inside, lining adj. inner, internal, interior
External adj.	internal, interior, inner inside
Extinct adj.	alive, present, extant, flourishing
Extinction n.	survival
Extinguish vb.	light
Extirpate vb.	establish
Extortionate adj.	moderate
Extract vb.	insert, introduce, penetrate
Extraneous adj.	intrinsic, relevant

Failure

Extraordinary adj.	ordinary, commonplace, usual
Extravagant adj.	frugal, economical, prudent, thrifty, provident
Extreme adj.	moderate, reasonable, modest

F

Fable n.	
Fabricate vb.	destroy, demolish, raze
Fabulous adj.	commonplace, ordinary
Face vb.	
Facile adj.	awkward, obdurate
Facilitate vb.	hinder
Facility n.	difficulty, effort, labour
Facsimile n.	original
Fact n.	fiction
Factitious adj.	genuine
Factual adj.	erroneous, invented, fabricated, incorrect, false
Faculty n.	inability
Fade vb.	increase, grow, wax, darken
Fag vb.	refresh
Fail vb.	succeed
Failure n.	success, achievement, accomplishment

Faint

Faint adj.	clear, sharp, distinct, strong, forceful, loud
Fainthearted adj.	brave, courageous, stouthearted, fearless
Fair adj.	unfair, unjust, biases, dark, dusky, swarthy, stormy, cloudy, threatening
Faith n.	mistrust, distrust, disbelief, doubt, faithlessness
Faithful adj.	disloyal, faithless, treacherous, inaccurate, erroneous, wrong
Faithless adj.	faithful, loyal
Fake adj.	genuine, real, authentic
Fall vb.	rise, soar, ascend, rise, increase, climb n. rise, ascent, increase
Fallacious adj.	true
Fallacy n.	truth
Fallible adj.	infallible
Follow adj.	cultivated
False adj.	true
Falsehood n.	truth
Falter vb.	decide
Fame n.	oblivion, anonymity
Famed adj.	unknown, anonymous, obscure
Familiar adj.	unfamiliar, unknown, foreign, alien, rare, distant, ignorant, unaware
Familiarity n.	ignorance, formality
Famine n.	plenty
Famished adj.	full

Famous adj.	unknown, obscure, anonymous
Fan vb.	quell
Fancy adj.	plain, unadorned, simple, undecorated
Fanciful adj.	realistic
Fantasy n.	reality
Far adj.	
Far-fetched adj.	believable, fundamental, basic
Father adj.	nearer
Farthest adj.	nearest
Fascinate vb.	bore
Fascination n.	repulsion
Fashionable adj.	unfashionable, dowdy
Fast adj.	slow, sluggish, loose, insecure
Fasten vb.	loosen, loose, free, release, unclasp
Fat adj.	thin, lean, emaciated, slim, scrawny
Fatal adj.	nonfatal, beneficial
Fathomless adj.	shallow
Fatigue n.	energy, vigor
Fatuity n.	sense
Fatuous adj.	sensible
Fault n.	
Faultless adj.	imperfect
Faulty adj.	perfect, flawless, whole
Favor vb.	disapprove, deplore
Favourable adj.	unfavorable, disapproving

Fierce adj.	gentle, peaceful, harmless
Fiery adj.	cool
Fight n.	peace
Fill vb.	empty
Filth n.	cleanness
Filthy adj.	clean, pure, spotless, unspoiled
Final adj.	first, initial, beginning, starting
Finale n.	beginning
Finally adv.	initially
Find vb.	lose
Fine adj.	inferior, poor, squalid, coarse, broad
Finesse n.	clumsiness
Finish vb.	begin, start, open **n.** opening, start, beginning
Finite n.	infinite
Firm adj.	limp, drooping, soft, weak, soft, squashy
First adj.	last **adv.** last
Fishy adj.	credible, believable
Fitting adj.	unsuitable, inappropriate, improper
Fix vb.	move, damage
Flabby adj.	firm
Flaccid adj.	firm
Flamboyant adj.	plain
Flare vb.	taper
Flash vb.	conceal

Flat adj.	uneven, rough, bumpy, interesting, stimulating
Flatter vb.	insult
Flaunt vb.	hide, conceal
Flee vb.	
Fleet vb.	slow, sluggish
Fleeting adj.	permanent, fixed, stable, lasting
Flexible adj.	inflexible, rigid, firm, unyielding, fixed
Flexuous adj.	straight
Flighty adj.	steady, solid, responsible
Flimsy adj.	strong, firm, stable
Flippant adj.	serious
Float vb.	sink
Flock vb.	disperse, scatter
Flop vb.	succeed **n.** success
Flourish vb.	decline, die
Flout vb.	respect
Flower vb.	wither
Flowing adj.	stilted, lacking
Fluctuate vb.	stabilize
Fluent adj.	stilted
Fluid n.	solid
Flurry n.	calm **vb.** compose
Fly vb.	remain
Foe n.	friend, ally
Foggy adj.	clear

Foil vb.	remain
Fold vb.	flatten, prosper
Follow vb.	flatten, precede
Follower n.	leader
Following adj.	preceding
Follow n.	wisdom
Fondness n.	unfriendliness, hostility, aversion
Foolish adj.	sensible, sound, reasonable, rational
Forbear vb.	indulge
Forbid vb.	allow, permit, let
Forbidding adj.	friendly, beneficent
Force vb.	coax, ease **n.** weakness
Forceful adj.	weak, namby-pamby
Force adj.	voluntary, natural
Fore n.	rear
Foreboding n.	reassurance
Foregoing adj.	following, below
Foregone n.	future
Foreign adj.	familiar, ordinary, commonplace
Foreigner n.	native, resident
Forerunner n.	successor
Foresight n.	improvidence
Forever adv.	temporarily, fleetingly
Foreword n.	epilogue
Forfeit vb.	earn **n.** reward
Gorged adj.	genuine, authentic
Forget vb.	remember

Forgive vb.	censure, blame, punish
Forgiveness n.	punishment
Fork vb.	unite
Forlorn adj.	happy
Form vb.	destroy, vanish, lose
Formal adj.	informal, unceremonious, unconventional
Formation n.	destruction
Former n.	present, current, future
Formidable adj.	reassuring
Forsake vb.	keep
Forthcoming adj.	previous, reticent
Forthright adj.	devious, tricky, evasive, roundabout
Fortitude n.	weakness
Fortuitous adj.	planned
Fortunate adj.	unlucky, cursed, unfortunate
Forward adv.	rearmost, last, shy, demure, retiring backward, rearward **adj.**
Foul adj.	clean, pure, immaculate, saintly, good, clear, sunny, calm
Found vb.	abolish, lose
Foxy adj.	naïve, artless
Fraction n.	whole
Fractious adj.	affable, docile
Fragile adj.	sturdy, hardy, strong, stout
Fragment n.	whole

Fragrant adj.	fetid, malodourous, noxious, smelly
Frail adj.	strong, sturdy, hardy, powerful
Frank adj.	devious, dishonest, tricky
Frantic adj.	calm, tranquil, composed
Fraud n.	honesty
Fraudulent adj.	honest
Fray n.	peace
Freakish adj.	normal, consistent
Free adj.	confined, busy, blocked, constrained **vb.** enslave, entrap, snare
Freedom n.	slavery, servitude, bondage, captivity, constraint
Freeze vb.	melt
Freezing adj.	hot
Frenetic adj.	calm
Frenzy n.	composure
Frequent adj.	infrequent, uncommon
Fresh adj.	old, out-of-date, impure, polluted, foul, exhausted, tired, stale, unoriginal, mature, seasoned, experienced
Fret vb.	soothe, calm
Fretful adj.	calm, easygoing
Friable adj.	tough
Friction n.	agreement
Friend n.	enemy, foe
Friendly adj.	unfriendly, hostile

Friendship n.	enmity
Fright n.	reassurance
Frighten vb.	reassure
Frigid adj.	warm
Fringe n.	centre
Frisky adj.	lethargic, lazy, sedate
Frivolous adj.	serious
Front n.	back, rear
Frosty adj.	hot, warm
Frown vb.	smile
Frown vb. phr.	approve
Frowzy adj.	neat
Frugal adj.	extravagant
Fruitful adj.	barren, lean, unproductive, fruitless
Fruitless adj.	fruitful, unproductive, fertile
Frustrate vb.	satisfy, gratify
Fuddled adj.	sober
Fugacious adj.	permanent
Full adj.	empty, vacant
Fully adv.	partly, inadequately
Fulsome adj.	meager
Fume vb.	calm
Fumigate vb.	infect
Fun n.	misery
Fundamental adj.	secondary
Funny adj.	unamusing, humorless, unfunny

Furbish vb.	tarnish
Furious adj.	calm, serene
Furl vb.	divest
Furnish vb.	divest
Furore n.	apathy, peace
Further adv.	nearer
Furtherance n.	hindrance
Furthest adj.	nearest
Furtive adj.	open, honest
Fury n.	serenity, calmness
Fuse vb.	separate
Fussy adj.	easygoing, placid
Fusty adj.	fresh, modern
Futile adj.	worthwhile, valuable, important, serious, weighty
Futility n.	usefulness, importance
Future n.	past, bygone, former
Fuzzy adj.	clear, lucid

G

Gaiety n.	depression, sadness
Gain vb.	lose n. loss
Gainful adj.	unprofitable
Gallant adj.	cowardly, churlish
Gallantry n.	cowardice, churlishness
Gallop vb.	amble

Gamble n.	certainty
Gape vb.	close
Garbled adj.	clear, straight
Gargantuan adj.	minute, tiny
Garish adj.	subdued, subtle, muted
Garner vb.	waste
Garrulous vb.	taciturn
Gather vb.	disperse, scatter, dispel
Gaudy adj.	muted
Gaunt adj.	plump
Gawky adj.	graceful
Gay adj.	sad, mournful, somber, sorrowful
Gaze vb.	glance
General adj.	definite, specific, exact, precise
Generosity n.	meanness
Generally adv.	rarely
Generate vb.	destroy
Generic adj.	specific
Generosity n.	meanness
Generous adj.	stingy, mean, selfish, tightfisted
Genius adj.	dunce, stupid **n.** stupidity
Gentle adj.	mean, nasty, rough, uncouth
Genuine adj.	fake, bogus, counterfeit, false, insincere, pretended, sham
Germinate vb.	wither, shrivel
Giant n.	dwarf, midget, runt **adj.** small, tiny, miniscule, infinitesimal

Gibberish n.	sense
Gigantic adj.	small, little, tiny, infinitesimal
Gingerly adv.	roughly
Give up vb. phr.	continue
Glacial adj.	hot, warm
Glad adj.	unhappy, sad, morose, gloomy, somber, dismal
Glamorous adj.	dull
Glance vb.	stare
Glare vb.	smile
Glaring adj.	concealed, muted
Glean vb.	scatter, disperse
Glee n.	sorrow
Gleeful adj.	sad, mournful
Glib adj.	hesitant
Glimpse n.	scrutiny **vb.** scrutinize
Glitter n.	dullness
Global adj.	restricted
Gloom n.	brightness, cheerfulness, happiness
Gloomy adj.	happy, cheerful, merry, highspirited, sunny, bright
Glorify vb.	defame
Glossy adj.	dull, matte
Glow n.	darkness, dullness
Glower vb.	smile
Glum adj.	happy, cheerful

Glut n.	dearth
Go vb.	come
Let go vb. phr.	hold
Goad vb.	deter, discourage
Go-ahead n.	ban
Good adj.	evil, bad, wicked
Good-looking adj.	ugly
Good-hearted adj.	evil-hearted
Governable adj.	wild
Graceful adj.	clumsy, awkward, gawky
Gradual adj.	sudden, swift, abrupt
Graft vb.	separate
Grand adj.	humble, modest, unassuming
Grandeur n.	humility
Grandiloquent adj.	simple
Grant vb.	deny, withhold
Grapple vb.	release
Grasp vb.	release
Grasping adj.	generous
Grate vb.	soothe
Grateful adj.	ungrateful, thankless, grudging
Gratification n.	frustration
Gratify vb.	frustrate, displease
Gratitude n.	ingratitude, thanklessness

Gravity n.	triviality
Great adj.	small, diminutive, insignificant, trivial, minor
Greed n.	generosity, selflessness, unselfishness
Greedy adj.	generous, giving, unselfish
Green adj.	decaying, experienced
Greeting n.	farewell
Grief n.	joy
Grieve vb.	rejoice, celebrate
Grievous adj.	commendable
Groggy adj.	alert
Groove n.	ridge
Gross adj.	refined, cultivated, polite
Groundless adj.	justified
Group vb.	separate, disarrange **n.** individual
Grow vb.	shrink, decrease
Growth n.	decline
Grubby adj.	clean
Gruff adj.	affable, friendly
Guard vb.	neglect, ignore, disregard
Guarded adj.	rash, careless, indiscreet
Guess vb.	know
Guest n.	host
Guide vb.	follow **n.** follower
Guile n.	honesty
Guileless adj.	plotting, treacherous

Guilt n.	innocence, impenitence
Guilty adj.	innocent, blameless, guiltless
Gullible adj.	sophisticated, skeptical
Gush vb.	drip
Guts n.	weakness

H

Habitual adj.	unusual, rare, occasional
Hackneyed adj.	original
Haggard adj.	fresh, animated, bright, clear-eyed
Haggle vb.	agree
Hail vb.	ignore
Hale adj.	frail, feeble, weak
Half n.	whole **adv.** completely
Half-hearted adj.	enthusiastic, eager, earnest
Hallow vb.	desecrate
Hallowed adj.	profane
Hallucination n.	reality
Halt vb.	proceed, start, begin **n.** start, beginning
Hamper vb.	assist
Hand over vb. phr.	retain
Handicap n.	advantage **vb.** assist

Handsome adj.	ugly, homely, unattractive, mean, petty, stingy, niggardly
Handy adj.	inconvenient
Haphazard adj.	orderly
Hapless adj.	lucky
Happiness n.	sadness, gloom, melancholy
Happy adj.	sad, gloomy, sorrowful, unlucky, inconvenient, unfortunate
Harbor vb.	expose, expel
Hard adj.	soft, pliable, yielding, easy, undemanding, comfortable, simple, uncomfortable, lenient, easygoing
Harden vb.	soften, loosen
Hard-hearted adj.	soft-hearted
Hardness n.	softness, easiness, tenderness
Hardship n.	prosperity
Hardy adj.	weak, feeble, frail, fragile, decrepit
Harm vb.	benefit **n.** good
Harmful adj.	beneficial, advantageous
Harmless adj.	harmful, injurious, dangerous
Hasten vb.	dawdle, linger, tarry
Hasty adj.	slow, thorough, cautious
Hate vb.	like, love, admire **n.** liking, love, esteem
Hateful adj.	lovable, likable, admirable, delightful
Hatred n.	liking, appreciation

Haughty adj.	humble, simple, down-to-earth, unaffected
Haughtiness n.	humility
Haul vb.	push
Hauteur n.	humility
Have vb.	lack, lose, forbid
Hazardous adj.	safe, secure
Hazy adj.	clear, definite
Head n.	foot, base, subordinate, end **vb.** follow
Headlong adv.	cautiously **adj.** cautious
Headstrong adj.	amenable, easygoing, tractable, prudent
Headway n.	retrogression
Heal vb.	aggravate, worsen
Healthy adj.	unhealthy, sick, ill, unwholesome
Heap vb.	scatter
Heartache n.	joy
Heartfelt adj.	insincere
Heartless adj.	kind, sympathetic
Heat n.	coolness, cold, coldness, itchiness, chilliness **vb.** cool, freeze, chill
Heavenly adj.	earthly
Height n.	depth
Heighten vb.	moderate, lower
Heinous adj.	admirable
Hell n.	heaven, ecstasy
Hello interj.	Goodbye, farewell, so long

Help vb.	hinder, aggravate n. hindrance, aggravation
Helper n.	opponent
Helpful adj.	useless, futile, worthless
Helpless adj.	component, resourceful, enterprising, strong
Herald vb.	suppress
Herd vb.	disperse, scatter
Hereditary adj.	acquired
Heroic adj.	cowardly, faint-hearted, timid
Heroism n.	cowardice, uncourageousness, timidity
Hesitate vb.	proceed
Hesitation n.	decision
Heterogeneous adj.	homogeneous
Hidden adj.	open
Hide vb.	show, display, reveal
Hideous adj.	beautiful, lovely, ethereal, beauteous
High adj.	low, short, lowly, deep, lowly, unimportant, insignificant, reasonable, inexpensive, petty, trivial
Highly adv.	badly, lowly
High-minded adj.	base, dishonourable
High-priced adj.	cheap, economical
High-stung adj.	calm

Hilarious adj.	serious, sad, depressing
Hinder vb.	help, promote, further, advance
Hindrance n.	assistance
Hire vb.	dismiss, fire
History n.	future
Hit vb.	miss
Hoard vb.	spend, use, squander
Hoarse adj.	clear, mellow
Hobby n.	profession, vocation, work
Hoist vb.	lower
Hold vb.	drop, release
Hollow adj.	full, filled, solid, sincere
Holy adj.	profane, unconsecrated, unsanctified
Homage vb.	disrespect
Homely adj.	attractive, beautiful, comely, pretty, handsome
Honest adj.	dishonest, fraudulent
Honesty n.	dishonesty, fraud
Honour n.	dishonour, disgrace, shame **vb.** dishonour, disgrace, shame
Honourable adj.	dishonourable, shameless, humiliating
Hook vb.	release, unhook
Hoot vb.	cheer
Hope n.	despair, hopelessness
Hopeful adj.	hopeless, despairing
Hopeless adj.	hopeful, promising
Horizontal adj.	vertical, upright

Horrible

Horrible adj.	wonderful, terrific, splendid
Horrify vb.	reassure
Hospitality adj.	unfriendliness, hostility
Host n.	guest
Hostile adj.	friendly, hospitable
Hostility n.	peace, friendliness
Hot adj.	cold, cool, chilly, freezing, bland, tasteless
Hotheaded adj.	coolheaded, levelheaded, calm
Hover vb.	decide
Huddle vb.	disperse
Huge adj.	small, tiny, diminutive, miniature
Hullabaloo n.	quiet
Human adj.	inhuman **n.** beast
Humane adj.	cruel, mean, heartless
Humble adj.	vain, proud, haughty
Humid adj.	dry
Humiliate vb.	dignify
Humility n.	hauteur, haughtiness
Humorous adj.	serious, unfunny, sober, somber
Hump vb.	straighten
Hunch vb.	straighten
Hungry adj.	full, sated, glutted, contented
Hunt vb.	find **n.** discovery
Hurried adj.	thorough
Hurry vb.	dawdle, linger, tarry **n.** leisure
Hurt vb.	soothe

Hurtful adj.	harmless
Husky adj.	weak, feeble
Hypocrisy n.	honesty, sincerity
Hypothesis n.	proof
Hysterical adj.	calm

I

Icy adj.	hot, warm
Idea n.	fact
Ideal adj.	imperfect, real
Idealistic adj.	realistic
Identical adj.	unalike, different
Idiocy n.	sense
Idle adj.	active, busy, occupied, engaged
Idolize vb.	despise
Ignite vb.	extinguish
Ignoble adj.	noble
Ignominious adj.	honourable
Ignoramus adj.	generous
Ignorance n.	knowledge, awareness
Ignore vb.	notice
Ill adj.	well, healthy, fit
Ill-advised adj.	wise
Ill-at-ease adj.	comfortable, at ease
Ill-bred adj.	polite
Illegal adj.	legal, lawful, legitimate

Illegitimate

Illegitimate adj.	legitimate, lawful
Ill-fated adj.	lucky
Illicit adj.	legal, licit, lawful
Illiterate adj.	literate, educated
Ill-mannered adj.	polite, courteous
Illness n.	fitness
Illogical adj.	logical, sensible
Illuminate adj.	darken, shadow, becloud, obscure
Illusion n.	reality, actuality
Illustrate vb.	obscure
Illustrious adj.	infamous
Ill will n.	goodwill
Imaginary adj.	real, actual
Imagination n.	reality
Imaginative adj.	unimaginative
Imagine vb.	know
Imbecile adj.	clever
Imitation n.	original
Immaculate adj.	dirty, impure
Immanent adj.	extrinsic
Immaterial adj.	important
Immature adj.	mature
Immeasurable adj.	limited
Immediate adj.	distant, long range, future
Immediately adv.	later
Immense adj.	small, tiny, miniscule, petite
Imminent adj.	past

Immobile adj.	mobile
Immodest adj.	bashful
Immoral adj.	virtuous
Immorality n.	virtue
Immortal adj.	perishable
Immortality n.	death
Immovable adj.	flexible
Immune adj.	susceptible
Immunity n.	liability
Impair vb.	improve
Impart vb.	suppress, withhold
Impartial adj.	biased, unfair, partial
Impassable adj.	penetrable
Impassive adj.	susceptible, passionate
Impeach vb.	vindicate
Impeccable adj.	imperfect
Impede vb.	assist
Impediment n.	aid
Impel vb.	deter
Impend vb.	pass
Imperative adj.	unimportant
Imperceptible adj.	unnoticeable
Imperfect adj.	perfect
Impersonal adj.	personal
Impertinent adj.	polite, courteous, respectful
Imperturbable adj.	agitated
Impervious adj.	permeable, receptive

Implant vb.	eradicate
Implicit adj.	explicit, outgoing
Implore vb.	demand
Imply vb.	state, declare
Impolite adj.	polite, courteous, respectful
Imposing adj.	insignificant, minor
Impossible adj.	possible
Impost n.	revenue
Impotent adj.	powerful
Impound vb.	free
Impoverished adj.	wealthy, rich
Impracticable adj.	possible, serviceable
Impregnable adj.	vulnerable, weak
Imprison vb.	release, free
Improbable adj.	likely
Impromptu adj.	prepared
Improper adj.	proper, fitting, appropriate
Improve vb.	impair, worsen
Improvement n.	deterioration
Impudent adj.	courteous, polite, respectful
Impure adj.	pure, chaste
Inaccurate adj.	accurate, correct, right
Inactive adj.	active, busy
Inadequate adj.	adequate, competent
Inadvertent adj.	intentional, deliberate
Inane adj.	sensible
Inanimate adj.	living, active

Inapt adj.	suitable, clever
Inattention n.	care
Inaugurate vb.	terminate
Inauspicious adj.	auspicious
Inborn adj.	acquired
Incandescent adj.	dull
Incapacitate vb.	enable
Incarcerate vb.	release
Incense vb.	pacify
Incentive n.	deterrent, discouragement
Inception n.	end
Incessant adj.	intermittent, irregular, essential
Incipient adj.	complete
Incisive adj.	mild
Incite vb.	deter, dissuade, discourage
Incline vb.	straighten
Inclined adj.	unlikely
Include vb.	exclude, omit
Income n.	expense
Incomparable adj.	ordinary
Incomprehensible adj.	understandable, plain
Inconceivable adj.	believable, conceivable
Inconsiderate adj.	considerate, thoughtful
Inconsistent adj.	consistent, logical
Inconspicuous adj.	conspicuous, obvious
Inconsolable adj.	cheerful

Inconstant adj.	steady, stable, constant
Incontestable adj.	dubious
Inconvenient adj.	convenient, handy
Incorporate vb.	sever
Incorrect adj.	accurate, proper, suitable
Incorruptible adj.	dishonest, perishable
Increase vb.	decrease, shrink, lessen, diminish **n.** decrease, lessening, shrinkage
Incredible adj.	credible, plausible, believable
Incredulity n.	belief
Increment n.	decrease
Incriminate vb.	vindicate
Inculpable adj.	guilty
Incumbent adj.	optional
Incur vb.	avoid
Incursion n.	retreat
Indecipherable adj.	legible
Indecision n.	resolution
Indefinite adj.	definite, decided, unequivocal
Indelible adj.	erasable
Independence n.	dependence, reliance
Indifferent adj.	concerned, caring, earnest
Indigenous adj.	exotic, acquired
Indignant adj.	serene, calm, content
Indirect adj.	direct, straight
Indiscernible adj.	visible

Indiscreet adj.	cautious
Indiscretion n.	caution
Indistinct adj.	clear, distinct
Indistinguishable adj.	different, conspicuous
Individual adj.	general n. group
Indolent adj.	vigorous, active, dynamic, zestful
Indomitable adj.	feeble, weak
Induce vb.	deter, prevent, dissuade, discourage
Inducement n.	discouragement
Induct vb.	oust, eject
Indulge vb.	deny
Indulgent adj.	severe, stern, strict
Indurate vb.	soften
Industrious adj.	lazy, indolent, shiftless
Inebriated adj.	sober
Inert adj.	active
Inertia adj.	activity
Inevitable adj.	avoidable
Inexorable adj.	indulgent
Inexpedient adj.	judicious
Inexpensive adj.	expensive, costly, dear
Inexperienced adj.	skilled, experienced, seasoned, trained, sophisticated
Inexpiable adj.	pardonable
Infamous adj.	illustrious

Infantile adj.	grownup, mature, adult
Infect vb.	sterilise
Infelicitous adj.	felicitous, appropriate
Inferior adj.	superior, higher, excellent
Infernal adj.	heavenly
Infidelity n.	faithfulness, belief
Infinite adj.	finite, limited
Infinitesimal adj.	enormous, huge, gigantic
Infirm adj.	strong, resolute
Infirmity n.	strength
Inflame vb.	calm, soothe, pacify, mitigate
Inflate vb.	deflate, collapse
Inflect vb.	straighten
Inflexible adj.	flexible, plaint, yielding, giving, elastic
Inflict vb.	spare
Influential adj.	insignificant
Infraction n.	observation
Infuriate vb.	pacify, soothe, calm
Ingenuity n.	stupidity
Ingrain vb.	eradicate
Ingredient n.	whole
Inhabit vb.	vacate
Inhabitant n.	visitor
Inherent vb.	bequeath
Inhibit vb.	encourage
Inhospitable adj.	hospitable, friendly
Inhuman adj.	humane

Inimical adj.	favourable
Iniquity n.	righteousness
Initial adj.	last, final, terminal
Initiate vb.	stop, finish, terminate, close
Injure vb.	benefit
Injurious adj.	beneficial, useful, advantageous
Injury n.	reparation
Inland n.	foreign
Innate adj.	acquired
Inner adj.	outer
Innocuous adj.	harmful
Innumerable adj.	few
Inopportune adj.	timely
Inquietude adj.	ease
Inquisitive adj.	uninterested, incurious
Insane adj.	sane, coherent, rational
Inscribe vb.	erase, delete
Inscrutable adj.	obvious
Insecure adj.	secure, stable, confident
Insensitive adj.	sensitive, caring
Insert vb.	extract
Inside adj.	external, outside n. surface adv. outside
Insidious adj.	straightforward
Insincere adj.	sincere, honest
Insinuate vb.	state
Insolent adj.	polite, courteous, deferential, respectful

Insolvent adj.	rich
Installation n.	ejection
Instantaneous adj.	slow
Instantly adv.	later
Instill vb.	eradicate
Instinct n.	reason
Institute vb.	terminate
Insufferable adj.	tolerable
Insult vb.	flatter, praise **n.** flattery, praise
Insurance n.	jeopardy
Insure vb.	imperil
Insurgent adj.	obedient
Intact adj.	broken
Integral n.	non-essential
Integrated adj.	segregated, separated, divided
Integrity n.	dishonesty
Intellectual n.	dunce, stupid
Intelligent adj.	stupid, slow, unintelligent, dumb
Intense adj.	mild, apathetic
Intensity n.	mildness
Intent adj.	indifference
Intentional adj.	accidental, chance
Intentionally adv.	accidentally
Interest n.	disinterest, apathy **vb.** bore, weary
Interlace vb.	unravel
Interminable adj.	brief

Intermingle vb.	separate
Intermission n.	continuance
Intermittent adj.	continuous
Internal adj.	external, outer, surface
International adj.	national
Interpolate vb.	delete
Interpret vb.	mystify
Interrupt vb.	continue
Intolerable adj.	tolerable, bearable
Intolerant adj.	tolerant, broadminded, fair
Intoxication n.	sobriety
Intricate adj.	simple, easy
Intrigue vb.	bore
Intrinsic adj.	extrinsic
Introduce vb.	end, withdraw, remove
Introduction n.	epilogue
Intuition n.	reason
Inundate vb.	drain
Invalid adj.	hale, healthy
Invalidate vb.	validate
Invaluable adj.	valuable, worthless
Invasion n.	retreat
Investigate vb.	ignore
Invigorate vb.	enervate
Inviting adj.	uninviting, unattractive
Involuntary adj.	voluntary, willing, willed, willful
Involve vb.	exclude, extricate

Inward adj.	outward, outgoing
Irate vb.	calm
Irascible adj.	affable, friendly
Irk vb.	please
Irksome adj.	pleasant
Irrefutable adj.	questionable
Irregular adj.	regular, even
Irrelevant adj.	relevant
Irresistible adj.	resistible, repulsive
Irritable adj.	affable, cheerful, happy
Irritate vb.	soothe, pacify, calm
Isolate vb.	unite
Issue vb.	withhold

J

Jade vb.	refresh
Jar vb.	agree **n.** harmony
Jaundiced adj.	fair
Jealous adj.	content
Jeer vb.	acclaim **n.** acclamation
Jeopardise vb.	secure, protect
Jocose adj.	melancholy
Jocular adj.	serious
Join vb.	split, separate, divide, sunder
Joint adj.	separate, divided
Jolly adj.	sad, somber, gloomy, melancholy

Joy n.	unhappiness, misery, sadness, gloomy, sorrow
Joyful adj.	sad, unhappy, gloomy
Jubilant adj.	mournful
Jubilation n.	mournful
Judgement n.	pleading
Juicy adj.	dry
Jumble vb.	arrange
Jump vb.	drop
Jumpy adj.	calm, tranquil, unruffled
Junction n.	division
Junior n.	senior
Just adj.	unjust, unfair, unmerited
Juvenile adj.	mature **n.** adult

K

Keen adj.	dull, blunted, dull, stupid, slow, obtuse, apathetic
Keep vb.	discard, cease, use, neglect, break
Kernel n.	shell
Kid n.	adult
Kin adj.	unrelated
Kind adj.	cruel, brutal, mean, hardhearted
Kindle vb.	extinguish, quell
Kindly adj.	cruel, mean **adv.** unkindly
Kindred adj.	unrelated

King n.	subject
Kingly adj.	lowly, squalid
Kink vb.	straighten
Knack n.	inability
Knavish adj.	honest
Knit vb.	separate
Knock down vb.	**phr.**
Knot vb.	untie
Knotty adj.	smooth, simple
Knowing adj.	unconscious, artless
Knowledge n.	ignorance
Kudos n.	disgrace

L

Laborious adj.	easy, simple, restful, relaxing
Labour n.	idleness, management **vb.** rest
Labyrinthine adj.	simple
Lacerate vb.	mend
Lack n.	abundance, quantity, plentifulness, profusion
Laconic adj.	verbose
Lad n.	lass
Lag vb.	hurry
Lame adj.	convincing, believeable, plausible
Lament adj.	rejoice
Languid adj.	spirited

Word	Meaning
Languish vb.	flourish
Languor n.	energy, enthusiasm
Lank adj.	fat, obese
Lapse n.	improvement, continuation vb. continue
Large adj.	small, little, tiny, diminutive
Largely adv.	partly
Largess n.	meanness
Lash vb.	untie
Last adj.	first, initial, starting, beginning vb. perish
Lasting adj.	transient
Late adj.	early
Latent adj.	conspicuous
Latitude n.	restriction
Latter adj.	former
Laudable adj.	contemptible
Laugh vb.	cry
Laughable adj.	serious
Launch vb.	stop, finish, terminate
Lawful adj.	unlawful, lawless
Lawless adj.	law-abiding, obedient, tame
Lax adj.	strict, alert
Lay vb.	remove, withdraw n. professional
Lead vb.	follow
Leader n.	follower, disciple
League vb.	part n. division
Leak vb.	conceal

Lean adj.	fat, portly, heavy, obese
Leap vb.	drop
Learn vb.	forget
Learned adj.	ignorant, uneducated, unlettered, illiterate
Learning n.	ignorance
Least adj.	most
Leave vb.	arrive, come
Leave out vb. phr.	include
Lecherous adj.	chaste
Legal adj.	illegal
Legendary adj.	historical, unknown
Legible adj.	illegible
Legitimate adj.	illegitimate, illegal, unlawful
Leisure n.	work
Leisurely adj.	hurried, pressed, forced, rushed, hasty
Lend vb.	borrow
Length adj.	briefly
Lengthen n.	breadth
At length adj.	briefly
Lengthen vb.	shorten, contract, shrink
Lengthy adj.	short
Lenient adj.	strict
Less adj.	more
Lethargic adj.	energetic, vivacious
Lethargy n.	vitality, energy

Lettered adj.	ignorant, illiterate, unlettered
Level adj.	uneven, unequal **vb.** build
Levity n.	seriousness
Lewd adj.	decorous
Liabilities n.	assets
Liberal adj.	narrow-minded, stingy, mean, tightfisted, selfish
Liberate vb.	confine, imprison, jail
Libertine n.	ascetic **adj.** chaste
Liberty n.	bondage, servitude, slavery
Licence n.	prohibition, restraint
Lie n.	trust
Life n.	death
Lifeless adj.	living, lively
Shift vb.	drop, lower, impose
Light n.	dark **vb.** darken, extinguish **adj.** dark
Lighten vb.	darken, encumber, depress
Likewise adv.	otherwise
Liking n.	dislike, aversion, antipathy
Limp adj.	stiff, rigid, hard
Limpid adj.	opaque, agitated
Link vb.	separate
Liquefy vb.	solidify
Liquid n.	solid
Listen vb.	ignore
Listless adj.	energetic, vivacious
Literal adj.	loose

Litter vb.	tidy n. tidiness
Little adj.	large, big, huge, long extended, ample, considerable n. lot
Live vb.	die
Lively adj.	slow, sluggish, dull
Livid adj.	calm
Living adj.	dead
Load vb.	unload
Loaded adj.	sober
Loan vb.	borrow
Loathe vb.	adore, lone
Loathsome adj.	attractive, alluring, delightful
Loathing n.	love, admiration
Local adj.	general
Locate vb.	remove
Lock vb.	unlock
Lodge vb.	remove
Lodger n.	landlord
Lofty adj.	lowly, low, humble
Logical adj.	irrational, illogical, crazy
Loiter vb.	hurry, rush
Long adj.	short, brief, limited
Loosen vb.	tighten, tie, secure
Loquacious adj.	taciturn
Lose vb.	find, discover, locate, place
Loss n.	gain
Lost adj.	found
Loud adj.	soft, quiet, subdued, murmuring

Lounge vb.	work
Loveable adj.	detestable, loathsome
Love n.	hate, loathing **vb.** hate, detest, loathe
Lovely adj.	ugly, hideous, horribly
Low adj.	high, happy
Lower vb.	increase, raise
Lowly adj.	noble, royal, lofty
Loyal adj.	disloyal, treacherous, traitorous, traitorousness
Lucent adj.	dark
Lucid adj.	unclear, unintelligible, opaque, muddy
Luck n.	misfortune
Lucky adj.	unlucky, unfortunate
Lucrative adj.	unprofitable
Lugubrious adj.	cheerful
Lukewarm adj.	cold, unenthusiastic
Lull vb.	disturb, increase
Luminous adj.	dark
Lunacy adj.	sanity
Lunatic adj.	sanc
Lure vb.	repel **n.** repulsion
Lurk vb.	emerge
Luscious adj.	revolting, repulsive
Lust n.	indifference, frigidity
Luster n.	dullness
Luxuriant adj.	sparse, simple
Luxuriate vb.	whither

Luxurious adj.	sparse, Spartan, austere, simple, crude
Luxury n.	austerity, necessity
Lying adj.	truthful

M

Mad adj.	sensible, sane, rational, lucid, happy, cheerful, content
Madden adj.	mollify, calm, please, pacify
Madness n.	sanity, composure
Magnanimous adj.	mean
Magnificent adj.	plain, simple
Magnify vb.	diminish, reduce
Magnitude n.	insignificance
Maiden adj.	secondary, accessory
Main adj.	minor
Mainly adv.	partly
Maintain vb.	discontinue
Maintenance n.	neglect
Majestic adj.	lowly, base, squalid
Major adj.	minor, inconsequential
Majority adj.	minority
Make vb.	destroy, undo, spend, prevent
Maladroit adj.	dexterous, skillful
Malady n.	fitness

Male n.	female, feminine, womanly
Malediction n.	blessing
Malice n.	benevolence, charity
Malign vb.	praise
Malignant adj.	benign
Mammoth adj.	small, tiny, miniscule
Manacle vb.	free
Manage vb.	mismanage, bungle, fail
Management n.	mismanagement, labour
Mandatory adj.	optional
Maniacal adj.	sane
Manifest adj.	hidden, concealed **vb.** hide
Manly adj.	womanly
Mannerly adj.	rude
Manual adj.	automatic
Many adj.	few
Mar vb.	improve
March vb.	halt
Marine n.	land
Marginal adj.	essential
Marriage n.	divorce, separation
Marry vb.	separate
Marshal vb.	disarrange
Marvelous adj.	commonplace, ordinary, usual
Masculine adj.	feminine, female, unmasculine
Mask vb.	expose
Mass vb.	disperse
Massive adj.	small, little, tiny, light, weightless

Master n.	servant, novice, pupil
Masterly adj.	clumsy, maladroit, awkward, inept
Match vb.	clash, separate
Matchless adj.	unimpressive, ordinary
Mate vb.	separate
Material adj.	immaterial, irrelevant, immaterial, intangible, spiritual
Mature adj.	young, youthful, immature, innocent, naïve
Maximum adj.	minimum
Maybe adv.	definitely, decidedly
Meager adj.	plentiful, bountiful, ample, abundant
Mean adj.	generous, openhanded, gentle, thoughtful, kind
Means n.	end
Measureless adj.	measurable, ascertainable, figurable
Mediocre adj.	excellent
Medium n.	extreme
Meet vb.	miss, diverge, split, scatter, disagree
Meeting vb.	parting, divergence
Melancholy adj.	happy, joyful, jubilant n. elation
Mellow adj.	immature, unripened
Melodious adj.	discordant
Melt vb.	harden, freeze, solidify
Memorable adj.	forgettable, passing, transitory, insignificant
Memorise vb.	forget
Memory n.	forgetfulness, oblivion

Mend vb.	ruin, destroy, spoil, damage, deteriorate
Mental adj.	physical
Mention vb.	omit
Merciful adj.	unjust, unforgiving, harsh, mean, vengeful, deteriorate
Merciless adj.	merciful, benevolent, openhearted
Mercy n.	cruelty, ruthlessness, pitilessness
Mere adj.	considerable, substantial
Merge vb.	separate
Merger n.	separation
Merit n.	fault
Merry n.	sad, gloomy, doleful
Mesh vb.	free
Messy adj.	neat, orderly, tidy
Method n.	disorder
Methodical adj.	disorganised
Meticulous adj.	slapdash
Middle n. adj.	beginning, end
Midst n.	edge
Might n.	weakness, frailty, vulnerability
Mighty adj.	weak, frail, tiny
Migrate vb.	remain, stay, settle
Mild adj.	stormy, turbulent, violent, excitable, harsh, hot-tempered
Mind vb.	ignore, neglect
Mingle vb.	separate, sort
Miniature adj.	outsize, large

Minimise vb.	maximize, enlarge
Minor adj.	minor **n.** adult, grownup
Minus adj.	plus
Minute adj.	large, huge, immense
Miraculous adj.	ordinary, commonplace, everyday
Mirth n.	gloom, sadness, seriousness, melancholy
Miscarry vb.	succeed
Miserly adj.	generous, openhanded, spendthrift, extravagant
Misery n.	delight, joy
Misgiving n.	assurance
Mislay vb.	find, discover
misprize vb.	value
Mistaken adj.	correct, right, accurate
Mistrust vb.	trust **n.** confidence
Misty adj.	clear
Mitigate vb.	aggravate, worsen, intensity
Mix vb.	separate, divide
Moan vb.	rejoice
Mob n.	individual
Mobile adj.	immobile, stationary, fixed
Mock vb.	praise, honour, applaud, respect, real, genuine, authentic
Mockery n.	praise, admiration
Moderate adj.	immoderate, excessive, heavy
Moderate vb.	intensify, increase, aggravate
Modern adj.	old-fashioned, antique, out-of-date, outmoded

Moor vb.	untie
Moral adj.	immoral, dishonest, sinful, corrupt
Morbid adj.	healthy
More adj.	less
Mortal adj.	immortal, superficial
Mortification n.	delight
Most adj.	fewest **n.** least
Motion n.	stillness, immobility
Motivate vb.	deter
Mouldy adj.	fresh
Mount vb.	descend, decrease
Mourn vb.	rejoice, celebrate
Mournful adj.	cheerful, joyful, happy
Movable adj.	fixed
Move vb.	stay, deter
Moving adj.	still
Much adj.	little
Muddle n.	order
Muddy adj.	clean
Muffle vb.	amplify, louden
Multiply vb.	decrease, lessen
Mundane adj.	superficial, deep, spiritual
Munificent adj.	mean
Murky adj.	clear
Mushroom vb.	decline
Musty adj.	fresh
Mutable adj.	constant
Mute adj.	loud

Mutilate vb.	mend
Mutinous adj.	obedient, dutiful, compliant
Myopic adj.	long-sighted
Mysterious adj.	open, direct, obvious, plain
Mystify vb.	enlighten
Myth n.	history, fact
Mythical adj.	historical, real

N

Nab vb.	release
Naive adj.	artful, clever
Naked adj.	covered, clothed, garbed, suppressed, concealed
Narcotic n.	stimulant
Narrow adj.	wide, broad **vb.** broaden
Nauseous adj.	pleasant
Narrow-minded adj.	broad-minded, liberal, tolerant
Nascent adj.	mature
Nasty adj.	pleasant, fair, seasonable, clean, pure, proper, decent, pleasant, even-tempered
National adj.	local
Native adj.	foreigner, alien **n.** stranger, foreigner, outsider
Natural adj.	unnatural, alien, contrary, acquired, artificial
Naturally adv.	artificially

Naughty adj.	untidy, good, well-behaved, obedient
Near adj.	far, distant, remote
Neat adj.	messy, sloppy, unkempt, disorganized
Necessary adj.	unnecessary, dispensable, unneeded
Necessity n.	luxury, wealth
Need vb.	have
Needy adj.	wealthy, well-to-do, affluent, well-off, well-heeled
Negate vb.	affirm
Negative n.	positive
Neglect vb.	care, attend n. attention, concern, regard
Neglectful adj.	attentive
Neglectful adj.	attentive
Neighbouring adj.	distant
Neighbourly adj.	unfriendly
Nerve n.	cowardice, weakness, frailty
Nervous adj.	calm, tranquil, placid, bold, courageous, confident
Nettle vb.	soothe, pacify, appease
Neutral adj.	partisan, biased
Neutralize vb.	intensify
New adj.	old, ancient, usual, outmoded
Nice adj.	unpleasant, disagreeable, nasty, thoughtless, unkind, careless, inexact

Niggardly adj.	generous, ample
Night n.	day
Nightfall n.	daybreak
Nimble adj.	clumsy, awkward, oafish
Noble adj.	ignoble, base, dishonest, lowborn
Nobody n.	somebody
Noise n.	quiet, silence, peace
Noiseless adj.	loud
Noisy adj.	quiet, silence, peaceful
Nominal adj.	excessive
Nonchalant adj.	concerned
Nondescript adj.	distinctive
Nonplus vb.	enlighten
Nonsense n.	sense
Nonsensical adj.	sensible
Normal adj.	abnormal, odd, irregular, peculiar
Notable adj.	ordinary, usual, commonplace, insignificant **n.** nobody
Note vb.	ignore
Noted adj.	unknown, anonymous
Noteworthy adj.	ordinary
Nothing adv.	something
Notice vb.	ignore, miss, disregard, overlook
Noticeable adj.	inconspicuous
Notify vb.	suppress
Notorious adj.	illustrious
Nourish vb.	deprive, starve

Nourishment n.	deprivation, starvation
Novel adj.	stale, old
Now adv.	later, then
Noxious adj.	beneficial
Nude adj.	clothed, garbed
Nugatory adj.	valuable
Nuisance adj.	pleasure
Numerous adj.	few, scanty
Nurse vb.	neglect, banish
Nutritious adj.	unhealthy

O

Obdurate adj.	amenable, complaint
Obedience n.	disobedience, rebellious
Obedient adj.	rebellious, mutinous, disobedient
Obeisance n.	disrespect
Obese adj.	slender, thin, lanky
Object vb.	approve, agree, assent
Objection n.	approval, agreement, assent, concurrence
Objectionable adj.	agreeable
Objective n.	subjective, biased
Objectivity n.	bias
Obligatory adj.	optional
Oblige vb.	disoblige, free

Oblique adj.	vertical, direct
Obliterate vb.	restore
Oblivion n.	awareness
Oblivious adj.	aware
Obscene adj.	decent
Obscure adj.	famous, noted, distinguished, clear, lucid, illuminated, bright
Observance n.	disregard, omission
Observant adj.	unobservant, inattentive
Observe vb.	ignore, disregard, miss
Obsolete adj.	modern, new, up-to-date, fashionable
Obstacle n.	aid, support, assistance
Obstinate adj.	pliable, pliant, yielding
Obstruct vb.	help, further
Obstruction n.	clearance
Obtain vb.	lose, forgo
Obtuse adj.	pointed
Obviate vb.	necessitate
Obvious adj.	subtle, hidden, unobtrusive
Occasional adj.	regular, chronic, constant
Offensive adj.	defensive, defending, pleasing, pleasant, agreeable, attractive n. refusal, denial
Offhand adj.	planned, considered, calculated, thought-out
Official adj.	unofficial

Offspring n.	parent
Often adv.	rarely, seldom, hardly
Okay adj.	unacceptable
Old adj.	young, youthful, fresh, brand-new
Old-fashioned adj.	new, up-to-date, fashionable, current, modern
Old-timer adj.	newcomer
Omit vb.	include
One adj.	many
Onerous adj.	light
One-sided adj.	impartial, just
Onset n.	end, conclusion, finale, retreat
Opaque adj.	transparent, clear, clever
Open adj.	closed, shut, sealed, private, secretive, filled, taken **vb.** finish, end, stop, close, clench
Operative adj.	inoperative
Opponent n.	ally, teammate, colleague
Oppose vb.	support
Opposite adj.	same, like, similar
Opposition n.	support, help, co-operation, agreement
Oppression n.	freedom, liberty
Oppressive adj.	mild
Optimism n.	pessimism, doubtfulness, cynicism
Optimistic adj.	pessimistic
Opulent adj.	poor, meager

Oral adj.	written, printed
Order n.	disorder, anarchy
Ordinary adj.	extraordinary, unusual, special
Organise vb.	disturb
Origin n.	end, termination, result
Original adj.	secondary, outmoded, old-fashioned **n.** copy
Originate vb.	abolish, end
Originator n.	imitator, follower
Ornate adj.	plain
Ostracize vb.	accept
Oust vb.	install
Outcome n.	cause
Outgoing adj.	incoming, unfriendly
Outlandish adj.	common, ordinary, conventional
Outmoded adj.	modern, up-to-date
Outrageous adj.	reasonable, sensible, prudent
Outset n.	end, climax
Outside n.	inside, interior
Outsider n.	insider, intimate
Outskirts n.	center
Outspoken adj.	reserved
Outward adj.	inward
Overcast adj.	clear, sunny
Overcome vb.	submit, yield
Overflow vb.	subside
Overjoyed adj.	upset

Overlook vb.	notice, note
Overpower vb.	surrender, submit, yield
Overpowering adj.	weak
Overrate vb.	underrate
Oversight n.	attention
Overt adj.	secret
Overthrow vb.	restore **n.** restoration

P

Pacific adj.	turbulent, excited, roiled
Pacify vb.	upset, irk, excite, disturb, aggravate
Pain n.	comfort, ease, relief, delight, joy
Painful adj.	soothing, pleasant
Painstaking adj.	careless, slipshod
Pair n.	individual **vb.** separate
Palatable adj.	unpleasant, tasteless **n.** composure
Pale adj.	ruddy, flushed, dark, bright
Paltry adj.	considerable, sufficient
Palliate vb.	aggravate, worsen, intensify
Panic vb.	calm, soothe, tranquilize **n.** composure
Parallel adj.	divergent
Paramount adj.	minor, insignificant
Parched adj.	flooded
Pardon vb.	condemn, sentence, punish

Parity

Parity n.	disparity
Part n.	whole, entirely
Partwith vb. phr.	retain, withhold
Partial adj.	entire, complete, comprehensive, fair, just, impartial
Particular adj.	general, ordinary
Parting n.	union adj. opening
Partition n.	joining, unification
Partner n.	rival
Pass vb.	stop, fail, withhold, reject, consider, notice, note
Passable adj.	exceptional, extraordinary, superior, excellent
Passé adj.	modern, up-to-date
Passion n.	indifference, apathy, coolness
Passionate adj.	apathetic, calm, frigid
Passive adj.	active
Past adj.	ahead, present, future n. present, future
Pastime n.	work
Patent adj.	hidden
Patience n.	impatience, restlessness, impetuosity
Patronise vb.	respect
Paucity n.	abundance
Pause n.	continuity, perpetuity vb. continue, proceed, perpetuate
Perpetuate vb.	proceed

Pave vb.	impede
Pawn vb.	redeem
Pay vb.	owe, withhold
Peace n.	agitation, upheaval, disturbance, war
Peaceable adj.	hostile, aggressive, warlike
Peaceful adj.	disrupted, agitated, riotous
Peak n.	base, bottom
Peculiar adj.	ordinary, regular, usual, unspecial, general
Peddle vb.	buy
Pedestrian adj.	unusual, fascinating, extraordinary, special
Peel vb.	cover
Pellucid adj.	opaque, unintelligible
Pelt vb.	drizzle
Penalise vb.	reward
Penalty n.	reward
Penchant n.	aversion
Penetrable adj.	impenetrable
Penetrating adj.	dull
Penniless adj.	rich, wealthy, prosperous, well-off
Pensive adj.	carefree
Penurious adj.	generous, rich, abundant
Penury n.	affluence, abundance
Perceptible adj.	imperceptible
Perception n.	ignorance
Perceptive adj.	slow, obtuse

Perfect adj.	imperfect, flawed, second-rate
Perfidious adj.	loyal, faithful
Perfunctory adj.	thorough
Perhaps adv.	definitely, absolutely
Peril n.	Safety, security
Perilous adj.	safe, secure
Perimeter n.	center
Periodic adj.	continuous
Periphery n.	center
Perish vb.	last
Perky adj.	lethargic
Permanent adj.	passing, temporary, inconstant, fluctuating
Permissible adj.	restrictive, prohibitive
Permission n.	restriction, prohibition
Permit vb.	forbid, prohibit, disallow
Pernicious adj.	beneficial, harmless
Perpendicular adj.	oblique, horizontal
Perpetual adj.	intermittent, inconstant, fluctuating
Perplex vb.	enlighten, simplify
Persevere vb.	lapse, desist, discontinue, stop, wave
Persist vb.	stop, desist
Persistent adj.	wavering, intermittent
Personal adj.	public, communal, general
Persuade vb.	dissuade, discourage, deter
Persuasive adj.	unconvincing, dubious

Pert adj.	bashful
Pertinent adj.	irrelevant
Perturbed adj.	composed
Pessimistic adj.	optimistic
Pestilent adj.	beneficial
Pet adj.	wild
Petrify vb.	reassure
Petty adj.	grand, vital, significant, generous, bighearted
Phenomenal adj.	ordinary
Philanthropic adj.	selfish
Phlegmatic adj.	energetic
Phony adj.	genuine, real
Physical adj.	mental, spiritual
Pick vb.	reject, leave
Pick up vb. phr.	drop
Picturesque adj.	ugly
Piece n.	whole
Piecemeal adv.	entire, whole, complete
Pious adj.	impious, irreligious, profane
Pinnacle n.	base
Pique vb.	please **n.** pleasure
Pitiless adj.	kind, kindly, gentle, compassionate
Pity n.	cruelty, pitilessness, vindictiveness
Pivotal adj.	unimportant, peripheral, side
Placate vb.	incense, irk, irritate

Plain adj.	fancy, elaborate, ornamental, pretty, beautiful, comely, disguised, hidden, unclear
Plane adj.	uneven
Plant vb.	uproot, remove
Play vb.	work
Play down vb. phr.	emphasize
Playful adj.	serious
Plea n.	accusation
Pleasant adj.	horrid, disagreeable, sour, nasty, difficult
Please vb.	offend, displease, annoy, vex
Pleased adj.	upset
Pleasing adj.	irritating, annoying
Pleasure n.	pain, discomfort, torment, obligation, duty, responsibility
Plentiful adj.	scare, rare, scanty
Plentitude n.	scantiness
Plenty adj.	need, want, scarcity
Plethora n.	scarcity
Pluck n.	cowardice
Plucky adj.	cowardly
Plug vb.	open
Plump adj.	slim, thin, skinny
Plus adj.	minus
Poetry n.	prose
Pointed adj.	blunt

Point-blank adv.	indirectly, vaguely
Pointless adj.	worthwhile
Poise n.	indelicacy, coarseness, boorishness, ineptitude, awkwardness, instability, uncertainty
Poison vb.	cleanse
Polish vb.	dull, tarnish
Polite adj.	rude, discourteous, uncivil
Pollute vb.	purify, clean, clarify
Pompous adj.	humble
Ponderous adj.	light
Popular adj.	unpopular
Populous adj.	deserted
Porous adj.	impermeable, impenetrable
Portentous adj.	trivial, insignificant
Portion n.	whole
Portly adj.	slim, thin, slender
Positive adj.	unsure, dubious, mixed-up, confused, negative, adverse
Possess vb.	lose
Possible adj.	impossible
Possibly adv.	certainly
Posterior n.	front
Posterity n.	ancestry
Postpone vb.	advance
Potent adj.	impotent, weak, powerless, feeble
Pour vb.	drizzle

Pout vb.	smile
Poverty n.	wealth, richness, comfort, abundance, fruitfulness
Powerful adj.	weak, powerless, ineffectual
Practical adj.	impractical, visionary
Practice n.	theory
Practiced adj.	inept, inexperienced
Praise vb.	disapprove, condemn, criticise n. criticism, negation
Preamble n.	epilogue
Precarious adj.	safe
Precede vb.	follow
Precedence n.	subordination
Preceding adj.	subsequent, following
Precious adj.	worthless
Precipitate adj.	cautious, considered, gradual
Precipitous adj.	gradual, cautious
Precise adj.	vague
Precision n.	vagueness
Predecessor adj.	successor
Predetermined adj.	open
Predilection n.	aversion
Predominant adj.	secondary, accessory
Preface n.	epilogue
Preferment n.	demotion
Pregnable adj.	fortified

Prejudice n.	impartiality, justice
Prejudiced adj.	impartial, just
Premature adj.	timely, late
Premeditate vb.	improvise
Preparatory adj.	final
Prepare vb.	destroy
Prescribe vb.	prohibit
Presence n.	absence
Present adj.	absent n. future
Present vb.	withhold
Preservation n.	destruction
Preserve vb.	squander, waste, use, destroy
Pressing adj.	trivial
Pressure n.	relaxation
Presume vb.	know
Presumption n.	knowledge, fact
Pretence n.	truth
Pretentious adj.	humble, simple, unpretentious
Pretty adj.	plain, ugly
Prevail vb.	lose, yield
Prevailing adj.	rare
Prevalent adj.	rare, infrequent
Prevent vb.	aid, help, allow, abet
Previous adj.	later, following, subsequent
Pride n.	humility, humbleness
Primarily adv.	secondarily
Primary adj.	secondary, minor

Prime adj.	inferior n. decline
Principal adj.	secondary, accessory
Principle n.	practice, unscrupulousness
Prior adj.	subsequent, later
Pristine adj.	defiled, impured
Private adj.	public, general
Prize vb.	undervalue, disregard, underrate n. penalty
Probable adj.	unlikely
Problem n.	solution
Proceed vb.	withdraw, retreat
Proceeds n.	Expenses
Proclaim vb.	suppress
Procure vb.	lose
Prodigious adj.	ordinary
Prodigy n.	dunce, stupid
Produce vb.	destroy, withhold
Productive adj.	wasteful, useless, unproductive
Profane adj.	sacred, reverent
Profession n.	avocation, hobby, pastime
Professional adj.	amateur
Proffer vb.	withhold
Proficient adj.	incompetent
Profit n.	loss, debit vb. lose
Profitable adj.	unprofitable, unproductive
Profound adj.	shallow, superficial
Profuse adj.	scanty

Profusion n.	lack
Progress n.	regression **vb.** regress, backslide
Prohibit vb.	allow, permit, help, encourage
Prolific adj.	sterile, unproductive
Prolong vb.	curtail
Prominent adj.	inconspicuous, insignificant, unimportant
Promising adj.	hopeless
Promote vb.	hinder, demote
Prompt adj.	laggardly, tardy, late, slow **vb.** deter
Prone adj.	unlikely, upright
Pronounce vb.	suppress
Pronounced adj.	indistinguishable, minor, unnoticeable, vague
Proof n.	conjecture
Propogate vb.	suppress
Proper adj.	improper, wrong
Propitious adj.	inopportune, inappropriate
Proportion n.	disproportion, whole
Propose vb.	withdraw
Proscribe vb.	wane, fail
Prosperous adj.	poor, impoverished
Prostrate adj.	erect **vb.** restore
Protect vb.	expose
Prototype n.	copy
Proud adj.	modest, humble
Prove vb.	refute
Provident adj.	reckless

Provisional adj.	absolute
Provoke vb.	appease, deter
Prowess n.	incompetence
Proximity n.	distance
Prudence n.	rashness, reckless, foolish, foolhardy
Prudish adj.	broad-minded
Psychological adj.	physical
Public adj.	private
Publish adj.	suppress
Pucker vb.	smooth
Puff vb.	deflate
Pull vb.	push, repel
Punctilious adj.	lax
Punctual adj.	late, tardy, laggardly
Punish vb.	reward
Puny adj.	sturdy, strong
Pure adj.	adulterated, mixed, dirty, foul, tainted, immoral, licentious
Puritanical adj.	permissive
Purity n.	impurity, corruption
Purpose n.	indecision
On purpose n. phr.	accidentally, unintentionally
Pursue vb.	abandon
Push vb.	pull, deter
Pushy adj.	meek
Put vb.	remove, withdraw

Put down vb. phr.	praise
Put off vb. phr.	advance, encourage
Put out vb. phr.	light, kindle
Put up vb. phr.	demolish
Putrid adj.	fresh
Puzzle vb.	enlighten
Puzzling adj.	enlightening

Q

Qualified adj.	disqualified
Qualm n.	ease
Quarrel vb.	agree **n.** agreement
Quarrelsome adj.	genial, even-tempered
Queer adj.	ordinary, intensify
Quench vb.	light
Querulous adj.	contend
Query n.	answer
Question n.	answer, solution **vb.** answer, reply, respond
Quick adj.	slow, sluggish, patient
Quicken vb.	deaden
Quickly adj.	adv. slowly
Quiescent adj.	active
Quiet adj.	noisy, loud, boisterous, perturbed, anxious, fitful

Quieten vb.	disturb
Quite adv.	partly, very
Quixotic adj.	practical

R

Rabble n.	aristocracy
Rabid adj.	calm, rational
Race vb.	dawdle, linger, dwell, amble
Racket n.	dull, quiet
Radiant adj.	dim, lusterless, dark
Radical n.	moderate
Rage n.	calmness
Ragged adj.	smooth
Raging adj.	calm
Rally vb.	disperse, deteriorate
Rampant adj.	controlled
Rancid adj.	fresh
Rambling adj.	coherent, straightforward
Random adj.	particular, specific, special
Rapt adj.	bored
Rapture n.	sorrow
Rare adj.	common, ordinary, usual, everyday
Rash adj.	considered, thoughtful, prudent, cautious
Ration vb.	withhold, squander
Rational adj.	irrational, insane, crazy
Rattle vb.	reassure

Ravage vb.	preserve
Ravel vb.	unravel, disentangle
Ravenous adj.	sated, contended
Raving adj.	composed, calm
Ravishing adj.	ugly, repulsive
Raw adj.	cooked, processed, experienced
Raze vb.	erect, build, construct
Readily adv.	reluctantly, hesitantly
Ready adj.	reluctant, hesitant
Real adj.	false, counterfeit, sham, bogus
Realistic adj.	unrealistic, idealistic
Reality n.	imagination, fantasy
Reap vb.	sow, plant, seed
Rear n.	front **vb.** lower
Reasonable adj.	irrational, insane, outrageous
Reassure vb.	perturb
Rebate n.	surcharge
Rebel vb.	conform
Rebellious adj.	submissive
Rebuke vb. n.	praise
Recall vb.	forget
Recede vb.	advance
Receive vb.	give, offer
Recent n.	old, dated, outdated, out-of-date
Recess[1] n.	projection
Recess[2] n.	gather, convene
Recipient n.	donor
Reciprocal adj.	one-sided

Reckless adj.	cautious
Recline vb.	stand
Recognise vb.	ignore
Recollect vb.	forget
Recommend vb.	disapprove, veto, discourage
Reconcile vb.	alienate, oppose
Recover vb.	deteriorate, lose
Recovery n.	relapse, loss
Recreation n.	work
Recruit vb.	dismiss **n.** veteran
Recuperate vb.	decline, deteriorate
Redeem vb.	surrender
Reduce vb.	increase, enlarge, swell, elevate, raise
Redundant adj.	essential
Refined adj.	rude, coarse, brutish
Reflect vb.	conceal
Reform vb.	deteriorate
Refrain vb.	tire, exhaust
Refrigerate vb.	heat
Refuse vb.	accept, allow
Refute vb.	confirm
Regain vb.	lose
Regard vb.	ignore
Regardful adj.	needless
Regimented adj.	free, loose, unstructured
Regress vb.	progress **n.** progression
Regret n.	satisfaction

Regular adj.	irregular, odd, unusual, abnormal
Reign vb.	submit
Rein vb.	indulge
Reject vb.	accept
Rejoice vb.	mourn
Relapse vb.	improve **n.** improvement
Relate vb.	suppress
Relative adj.	absolute
Relax vb.	tighten, increase, intensify
Relaxation n.	work
Release vb.	hold, suppress **n.** imprisonment
Relegate vb.	reinstate
Relevant adj.	irrelevant
Reliable adj.	unreliable, erratic, eccentric
Relief n.	aggravation
Relieve vb.	aggravate
Religious adj.	irreligious, impious, lax, slack, indifferent
Relinquish vb.	retain
Relish vb.	distaste, disfavour
Reluctant adj.	ready, eager
Rely vb.	distrust
Remain vb.	depart, leave, go
Remarkable adj.	average, ordinary, commonplace
Remedy vb.	aggravate
Remember vb.	forget
Remote adj.	near, nearby, close

Remove vb.	replace
Removed adj.	involved
Render vb.	withhold
Renounce vb.	retain, acknowledge
Renown n.	anonymity, obscurity
Repair vb.	damage
Reparation n.	injury
Repeal vb.	enact
Repel vb.	attract, lure
Repentant adj.	unrepentant, satisfied
Repetition n.	originality
Replace vb.	remove
Replenish vb.	exhaust
Replete adj.	empty
Replica n.	original
Reply n.	**vb.** question
Repose n.	activity, agitation **vb.** work
Reprehend vb.	praise
Repress vb.	release
Reprimand vb.	commend
Repulsive adj.	attractive, delightful
Reputable adj.	disreputable
Requisite adj.	non-essential, optional
Rescue vb.	abandon, endanger
Resemblance n.	dissimilarity
Resentment n.	satisfaction
Reserve vb.	squander, waste
Reserved adj.	abandoned, wild, uninhibited, frank

Resign vb.	retain
Resist vb.	yield
Resolute adj.	wavering, irresolute, vacillating
Resolve vb.	waver
Resonant n.	quiet
Respect vb.	disrespect, disregard
Respectable adj.	disreputable, unsavoury
Restful adj.	disturbed, upsetting, tumultuous, agitated
Restless adj.	calm, tranquil, peaceful, restful
Restore vb.	remove
Restrain vb.	release
Restrict vb.	free
Restriction n.	freedom
Result n.	cause
Resume vb.	stop
Resurrection n.	extinction
Retain vb.	relinquish, free, release
Retaliate vb.	forgive
Retard vb.	advance, speed, accelerate
Retarded adj.	advanced, quick
Reticent adj.	forthcoming, talkative, garrulous
Retire vb.	advance, attack
Retiring adj.	bold, impudent, forceful
Retract vb.	confirm
Ridiculous adj.	sensible, sound
Rift n.	reconciliation

Right adj.	wrong, incorrect, fallacious, inappropriate
Rigid adj.	flexible
Rigorous adj.	lax
Rile vb.	pacify, soothe
Rinse vb.	dry
Riot n.	order, calmness
Rip vb.	mend
Ripe adj.	immature, ingrown
Rise vb.	fall, descent
Risible adj.	serious
Risk n.	safety
Risky adj.	safe, secure
Rival n.	ally
Roar n.	murmur
Rob vb.	endow
Robe vb.	strip
Rogue n.	gentleman
Romance n.	fact
Romantic adj.	realistic, down-to-earth
Roomy adj.	narrow
Rot vb.	preserve
Rotten adj.	fresh
Rotund adj.	angular, slim
Rough adj.	smooth, sleek, suave, sophisticated
Round adj.	angular, evasive
Round up vb.	disperse
Rouse vb.	soothe

Rout n.	victory
Routine adj.	uncommon, rare, unusual
Rove vb.	settle
Row n.	harmony
Rowdy adj.	quiet
Royal adj.	low-born, lowly
Rubbish n.	sense
Rude adj.	courteous, polished, cultivated
Ruffle vb.	smooth, compose
Rugged adj.	smooth
Ruin vb.	restore, fix
Ruinous adj.	beneficial
Rule n.	exception
Ruler n.	subject
Rumour n.	truth
Rumple vb.	smooth
Rural adj.	urban, citified
Rush vb.	dawdle, linger, tarry
Rustic adj.	sophisticated, refined, cultivated, urban
Ruthless adj.	compassionate

S

Sack vb.	appoint
Sacred adj.	profane, blasphemous
Sacrifice n.	gain
Sacrilege n.	reverence

Sad adj.	happy, joyous
Sadden vb.	cheer
Saddle vb.	relieve
Safe adj.	dangerous, risky
Safeguard vb.	imperil
Sag vb.	rise
Sagacious adj.	stupid
Salacious adj.	pure
Sale n.	purchase
Salubrious adj.	unhealthy
Salute vb.	ignore
Salvage vb.	destroy
Salvation n.	destruction
Salve vb.	aggravate, worsen
Same adj.	different
Sanction n.	prohibition
Sanctity n.	profanity
Sane adj.	insane, irrational, crazy
Sanguine adj.	pessimistic
Sanitary adj.	dirty, unclean, fouled, soiled
Sap vb.	strengthen
Satanic adj.	angelic
Satiate vb.	starve
Satisfaction n.	dissatisfaction
Satisfactory adj.	unsatisfactory, poor
Satisfy vb.	dissatisfy
Saturate vb.	drain

Saturnine adj.	jovial
Saucy adj.	demure, shy, respectful
Saunter vb.	hasten, run
Savage adj.	tame, cultivated
Savant adj.	stupid, irrational
Save vb.	abandon, expose, squander
Savoury adj.	insipid
Say vb.	suppress
Scale vb.	descend
Scanty adj.	plentiful, abundant, ample
Scarce adj.	common, usual, plentiful
Scarcity n.	abundance
Scare vb.	reassure
Scathing adj.	pleasant
Scatter vb.	gather, collect, assemble
Scoff vb.	respect
Scold vb.	praise
Scorn vb.	respect
Scornful adj.	respectful
Scowl vb.	smile
Scramble vb.	dawdle
Scrap n.	mass **vb.** keep
Scrawny adj.	burly, husky
Scream vb.	whisper
Screen vb.	expose
Scrimp vb.	lavish, squander
Scrub vb.	soil

150 Scrupulous

Scrupulous adj.	careless, lax
Scurry vb.	amble, saunter
Search n.	discovery
Seasoned adj.	novice, inexperienced
Secluded adj.	public
Second adj.	first **vb.** oppose
Secondary adj.	primary
Secret adj.	open, public
Secrete vb.	absorb
Sectarian adj.	broad-minded
Section n.	whole
Secure adj.	loose, free, endangered, insecure, vulnerable
Security n.	danger, insecurity
Sedative n.	stimulant
Sedentary adj.	active
Seek vb.	find, fail
Seemingly adv.	actually
Seemly adj.	unseemly, unattractive
Segment n.	whole
Segregate vb.	combine, unite, include
Seize vb.	release, loosen, drop
Seizure n.	release
Seldom adv.	often
Selfish adj.	Altruistic
Sell vb.	buy
Send vb.	retain

Senior adj.	junior, minor
Sensation n.	apathy
Sensible adj.	foolish, stupid
Sensitive adj.	insensitive, unfeeling
Sentence vb.	acquit
Sentiment n.	reason
Sentimental adj.	realistic
Separate vb.	mix, join
Sequence n.	disorder
Serene adj.	agitated, turbulent, stormy
Serious adj.	frivolous, light, jocular
Serpentine adj.	straight
Servant n.	employer
Serve vb.	command
Set vb.	move, change, melt
Set back vb. phr.	advance
Set off vb. phr.	arrive
Set up vb.	abolish
Settle vb.	migrate
Severe adj.	lenient, easygoing, mild
Shade n.	light **vb.** expose
Shadowy adj.	clear, distinct, bright
Shady adj.	honest, light
Snaggy adj.	smooth
Shaky adj.	definite, sure, certain, positive, firm

Shallow adj.	deep
Sham adj.	genuine
Shame n.	pride, honour
Shameful adj.	honorable
Shameless adj.	modest, demure
Shapely adj.	shapeless
Share n.	whole
Sharp adj.	blunt, gentle, mild, stupid, dull
Shatter vb.	mend, restore
Shed vb.	retain
Sheen n.	dullness
Shelter vb.	expose
Shield vb.	expose
Shift vb.	fix, stay
Shifty adj.	honest
Shiftless adj.	energetic
Shimmer n.	dullness
Shiny adj.	dull, lusterless
Shipshape adj.	messy, sloppy, untidy
Short adj.	long, lengthy, tall
Shortage n.	surplus, glut
Shortcoming n.	strength
Shorten vb.	lengthen
Shortly adv.	later
Shout vb.	whisper
Shove vb. n.	push

Show vb.	conceal
Chow up vb.	leave
Showy adj.	subdued
Shred n.	whole
Shrewd adj.	stupid
Shrill adj.	muted, muffled, low
Shrink vb.	swell, expand
Shrivel vb.	swell
Shroud vb.	expose
Shuffle vb.	sort
Shut vb.	open
Shut in vb. phr.	release
Shut out vb. phr.	admit
Shy adj.	bold, self-confident, brazen
Sick adj.	well
Sicken vb.	please
Sickness n.	health
Side n.	center **vb.** oppose **adj.** main
Sight n.	blindness **vb.** miss
Significant adj.	unimportant, insignificant, trivial
Silence n.	noise, noisiness, clamour, racket
Skillful adj.	inept, clumsy, awkward
Skill n.	ineptitude
Skim vb.	penetrate
Skimpy adj.	generous, abundant
Skinny adj.	plump, fat, heavy, hefty

Skittish

Skittish adj.	steady
Slack adj.	taut, stiff, rigid, active, busy
Slacken vb.	tighten
Slander vb.	praise
Slash vb.	mend, raise
Slave n.	master
Slavery n.	freedom, independence
Slay vb.	save
Sleep vb.	wake **n.** wakefulness
Sleepy adj.	alert
Slender adj.	heavy, fat, overweight
Slight adj.	large, enormous, huge, major, significant **vb.** flatter, complaint
Slim adj.	fat
Slipshod adj.	careful
Slit vb.	mend **n.** seam
Slothful adj.	industrious, energetic
Slovenly adj.	neat, meticulous
Slow adj.	fast, quick, prompt, fast, ahead
Sluggish adj.	energetic, vivacious, quick
Slump vb.	rise **n.** boom
Sly adj.	artless, honest
Small adj.	large, big, enormous, ample
Smart adj.	stupid, slow, dumb
Smile n.	**vb.** grin
Smooth adj.	rough, uneven
Smother vb.	revive

Snare vb.	free, release
Snatch vb.	release
Sneer vb.	admire **n.** respect
Snobbish adj.	humble
Snub vb.	flatter
Snug adj.	exposed
Soak vb.	dry
Soar vb.	sink
Sob vb.	laugh
Sober adj.	drunk, inebriated, fuddle, frivolous
Sobriety n.	drunkenness
Sociable adj.	unsociable
Social adj.	personal, unsocial
Society n.	privacy, commonalty
Soft adj.	hard, coarse, harsh, severe, rigid
Soil vb.	clean
Sojourn vb.	travel
Solemn adj.	cheerful, happy, gay
Solicitous adj.	indifferent
Solid adj.	loose
Solidarity n.	dissent
Solidify vb.	melt
Solution n.	problem
Solve vb.	complicated
Somber adj.	happy, cheerful, gay, bright
Sometimes adj.	always, invariably, never
Soon adj.	later

Soothe

Soothe vb.	disquiet, upset, unnerve, irritate
Sophisticated adj.	uncouth, primitive
Sore adj.	pleased
Sorrow n.	joy **adj.** rejoice
Sorrowful adj.	joyful
Sorry adj.	glad, happy
Sort vb.	muddle
Sound[1] n.	silence
Sound[2] adj.	faulty, unreliable
Soundless adj.	noisy
Sour adj.	sweet, good-natured, sunny, benevolent, genial
Sovereign n.	subject
Sow vb.	reap
Spacious adj.	cramped, narrow, confined, small
Spare vb.	punish, keep
Sparing adj.	lavish
Sparkle n.	dullness
Sparse adj.	dense
Spasmodic adj.	regular
Special adj.	average, ordinary
Specific adj.	general, nonspecific
Spectacular adj.	ordinary
Spectator n.	participant
Speculate vb.	know
Speculation n.	reality, fact

Speechless adj.	talkative
Speed n.	slowness
Speedy adj.	slow
Spend vb.	save, hoard
Spendthrift adj.	miser
Sphere adj.	square, cube, not-round
Spicy adj.	insipid
Spineless adj.	strong, brave, courageous, bold
Spiral adj.	straight
Spirited adj.	lazy, indolent, sleepy
Spiritual adj.	physical, profane
Spiteful adj.	benevolent
Splendid adj.	poor
Split vb.	poor
Split vb.	unite **n.** union
Spoil vb.	improve
Spontaneous adj.	studied, planned, cautious
Sport n.	work
Spot n.	miss, clean
Spotless adj.	impure, untidy
Spotty adj.	even, regular
Spread vb.	suppress, fold
Sprightly adj.	lifeless
Spring vb.	end
Spring up vb. phr.	disappear
Spry adj.	inactive, lethargic, sluggish

158 Spur

Spur vb.	deter n. deterrent
Spurious adj.	genuine, fake
Spy vb.	miss
Squabble n.	agreement
Squalid adj.	clean
Squander vb.	save, board
Stable adj.	unstable, shaky
Stagnant adj.	flowing, moving
Staid adj.	frivolous
Stale adj.	fresh, nes
Stand vb.	lie, recline, repose
Stand by vb. phr.	abandon
Stand for vb. phr.	oppose
Standard adj.	unusual, irregular, special
Stare vb.	ignore
Stark adv.	partially
Start vb.	finish, end
Startle vb.	compose
State vb.	suppress
Stately adj.	mean, base, squalid
Station vb.	move
Stationary adj.	mobile
Staunch adj.	wavering
Stay vb.	go, leave, depart
Steadfast adj.	wavering
Steady adj.	unsteady, irregular
Steal vb.	return

Stealthy adj.	open, direct, obvious
Steep adj.	gradual, moderate
Stench n.	perfume
Step up vb. phr.	reduce
Sterile adj.	fruitful
Stern adj.	lenient, forgiving
Stick vb.	separate
Sticky adj.	dry, fresh
Stiff adj.	limp, lax, warm, hospitable, lenient
Still adj.	agitated **n.** noise **vb.** agitate, disturb, upset
Stimulate vb.	deter
Stimulus n.	deterrent
Sting vb.	soothe
Stingy adj.	generous, open-handed, giving
Stint vb.	lavish
Stir vb.	stay **n.** tranquility
Stirring n.	dull
Stony adj.	warm
Stop n.	continuation
Store vb.	consume
Storm n.	calm
Stormy n.	still
Story n.	fact
Stout adj.	slim, thin, skinny, lean, flimsy
Straight adj.	crooked, twisted, dishonest
Straightaway adv.	later

Straightforward adj.	devious, deceitful
Strain n.	relaxation **vb.** relax
Strand vb.	rescue
Strange adj.	familiar
Stranger n.	friend, acquaintance
Strap vb.	loose
Strength n.	weakness, frailty
Strengthen vb.	weaken
Strenuous adj.	feeble
Stress n.	relaxation
Stretch vb.	contract, shrink
Strict adj.	lenient, easygoing
Strident adj.	soft
Strife n.	peace, tranquility, concord
Striking adj.	ordinary, commonplace
Stringent adj.	lax
Strip vb.	cover
Stroll vb.	run
Strong adj.	weak, feeble, fragile, bland, tasteless
Struggle vb.	yield
Stubborn adj.	amenable, pliable, fielding
Studied adj.	spontaneous
Study vb.	ignore
Stunning adj.	ugly, drab
Stupendous adj.	ordinary
Stupid adj.	intelligent, smart, quick, bright

Sturdy adj.	frail, flimsy, weak
Stylish adj.	dowdy
Submerge vb.	rise, surface
Submit vb.	resist, fight
Subside vb.	erupt, rise, increase
Subsidiary adj.	primary
Subsist vb.	die
Substantial adj.	trivial, important
Subtle adj.	obvious, overt
Subtract vb.	add
Subvert vb.	conserve
Succeed vb.	fail, flop, precede
Success n.	failure
Succulent adj.	dry
Succumb vb.	resist
Sudden adj.	gradual
Sue vb.	defend
Sufficient adj.	deficient
Suffuse vb.	drain
Suffix n.	prefix
Suitable adj.	inappropriate, unsuitable
Sullen adj.	cheerful, cheery, jovial
Sultry adj.	cool
Sum n.	part
Summit n.	base, bottom
Summon vb.	dismiss
Superb adj.	poor, awful

Superfluity n.	lax
Superior adj. n.	inferior
Supine adj.	upright, energetic
Supple adj.	stiff
Supplement vb.	reduce
Supplicate vb.	demand
Supply vb.	withhold, retain
Support vb.	drop, oppose, refute **n.** opposition
Supporter n.	opponent
Suppose vb.	know
Supposition n.	knowledge
Supremacy n.	subjection
Sure adj.	doubtful, precarious
Surface n.	interior
Surfeit n.	deficiency
Surge vb.	ebb, wane, diminish
Surly adj.	affable, friendly
Surmise n.	knowledge **vb.** know
Surplus adj.	deficit
Surrender vb.	resist, hold
Suspect vb.	know, believe, trust
Suspend vb.	continue
Suspicious adj.	trustful
Sustain vb.	drop, overrule
Sustenance n.	starvation
Swallow vb.	vomit
Swarm vb.	scatter

Swarthy adj.	pale
Swathe vb.	unwrap
Swear vb.	deny
Sweet adj.	sour, bitter, discordant, harsh, irritable, nasty, irascible
Swell vb.	shrink, diminish
Swift adj.	slow, sluggish, laggardly
Sympathy n.	indifference, antipathy
Synthetic adj.	genuine
System n.	chaos, disorder
Systematic adj.	random, irregular

T

Taboo adj.	permitted
Taciturn adj.	talkative, garrulous
Tactful adj.	tactless, unfeeling
Tactless adj.	tactful
Tail n.	head
Taint vb.	purify
Take vb.	give, leave, replace
Take in vb. phr.	exclude
Take on vb. phr.	dismiss
Take up vb. phr.	stop
Talent n.	inability
Talkative adj.	taciturn, silent, reticent
Tall adj.	short, low

Tame adj.	wild, exciting
Tangle vb.	untangle, unravel
Tantalize vb.	satisfy
Tardy adj.	prompt, punctual, timely
Tarnish vb.	polish
Tarry vb.	move
Tart adj.	sweet, sugary, mild
Task n.	leisure
Taste n.	aversion
Tasteless adj.	tasty, tasteful
Tasty adj.	insipid
Taut adj.	slack, loose
Tax vb.	relieve
Tear vb.	mend
Tease vb.	pacify, appease
Tedious adj.	interesting, engaging, exciting
Teeming adj.	empty
Tell vb.	suppress
Temerity n.	timidity, cowardice
Temper n.	calmness, rage **vb.** intensity
Temperamental adj.	serene, unruffled
Tempest n.	calm, peace, placid
Tempestuous adj.	calm, tranquil
Temporal adj.	spiritual, permanent
Temporary adj.	everlasting, permanent, fixed
Tempt vb.	repel

Tempting adj.	repulsive
Tenant n.	landlord
Tend vb.	neglect
Tendency n.	aversion
Tender adj.	tough, chewy, unfeeling, cruel, harsh
Tenderhearted adj.	hard-hearted, cruel
Tense adj.	Relaxed, lax **vb.** relax
Tentative adj.	sure
Tenuous adj.	substantial
Terminate vb.	begin, commence, start
Termination n.	beginning
Terrible adj.	wonderful
Terrific adj.	ordinary
Terrify vb.	reassure
Testify vb.	deny
Testy adj.	genial
Tether vb.	loose
Thankful adj.	ungrateful
Thankless adj.	grateful, rewarding
Thanks n.	ingratitude
Thaw vb.	freeze, solidify
Theoretical adj.	practical
Theory n.	practice
Therefore adv.	because
Thick adj.	thin, slim, watery
Thicken vb.	thin

Thin

Thin adj.	fat, thick **vb.** thicken
Thirsty adj.	satisfied
Thorny adj.	smooth
Thorough adj.	superficial, careless, haphazard, slapdash
Thoroughfare n.	byway
Thoughtful adj.	thoughtless
Thralldom n.	freedom, independence
Threaten vb.	reassure
Threshold n.	end
Thrift n.	extravagance
Threshold n.	end
Thrifty adj.	spendthrift, prodigal
Thrill vb.	bore
Thrive vb.	languish, expire, die
Throw vb.	catch
Throw away vb. phr.	keep
Tie vb.	untie, free
Tight adj.	loose, slack, sober, generous
Tilt vb.	straighten
Timely adj.	inopportune
Timid adj.	bold, forward, self-confident
Tiny adj.	large, huge, enormous
Tip n.	base
Tipsy adj.	sober
Tire vb.	refresh, exhilarate
Tired adj.	refreshed

Tiresome adj.	interesting, pleasant
Together adv.	separately
Toil vb.	relax, loll **n.** rest
Tolerant adj.	intolerant, biased, bigoted, prejudiced
Tone down vb. phr.	enhance
Top n.	bottom, base **adj.** lowest
Torment n.	relief
Torrent n.	trickle
Torrid adj.	frigid
Torture vb.	soothe
Total n.	part
Touchy adj.	calm, collected
Tough adj.	tender, weak, simple, vulnerable
Tow vb.	push
Toxic adj.	harmless, beneficial
Tragic adj.	comic
Trail vb.	catch
Traitor n.	loyalist
Tranquil adj.	disturbed, upset, agitated
Transgress vb.	obey
Transient adj.	permanent, everlasting
Transitory adj.	permanent, everlasting
Transmission n.	reception
Transparent adj.	opaque, unclear
Traverse vb.	assist

Treachery n.	loyalty, steadfastness
Treason n.	allegiance
Treat vb.	neglect
Tremendous adj.	small, ordinary
Tremulous adj.	steady
Trepidation n.	composure
Trail n.	relief
Tricky adj.	simple, artless
Trickle vb.	gush
Trifling adj.	important, significant
Triumph n.	defeat, failure
Triumphant adj.	beaten, defeated
Trivial adj.	important, significant
Troop vb.	disperse
Trouble n.	relief **vb.** soothe
Trying adj.	easy
Tug vb.	push
Tumult n.	peacefulness, tranquility
Tune vb.	discord
Turbid adj.	clear
Turbulent adj.	calm, composed
Turmoil n.	peace
Turn down vb. phr.	raise
Turn out vb. phr.	admit
Turn up vb. phr.	lower
Turncoat n.	loyalist

Twin adj.	single
Twine vb.	unravel
Two-faced adj.	honest, straight-forward
Typical adj.	atypical, odd, abnormal
Tyranny n.	democracy

U

Ugly adj.	beautiful pleasant, attractive
Ultimate adj.	first
Ultra adj.	moderate
Unaccountable adj.	understandable
Unaccustomed adj.	familiar
Unadorned adj.	ornate
Unadulterated adj.	mixed
Unaffected adj.	artificial
Unaided adj.	assisted
Unanimity n.	dissent
Unapproachable adj.	vulnerable, weak
Unassuming adj.	ostentatious, vain, showy, pompous, arrogant
Unattached adj.	attached
Unawares adj.	deliberately, knowingly, intentionally
Unbalanced adj.	sane
Unbending adj.	flexible
Unbidden adj.	forced, welcome
Unbounded adj.	limited

Unbridled adj.	restrained
Uncanny adj.	ordinary
Unceasing adj.	intermittent
Unceremonious adj.	formal
Uncertain adj.	certain, positive, unmistakable, sure
Unchanging adj.	transitory
Uncivil adj.	civil, polite
Unclean adj.	clean, tidy, pure
Uncomfortable adj.	relaxed, comfortable
Uncommon adj.	usual, ordinary
Uncommunicative adj.	talkative
Uncompromising adj.	pliant
Unconscious adj.	conscious, aware
Uncouth adj.	civilized, cultivated, cultured, refined
Unctuous adj.	sincere
Undaunted adj.	afraid
Undecided adj.	sure, settled
Undeniable adj.	questionable
Under prep.	above, over
Undercover adj.	public
Underestimate vb.	overestimate
Underhand adj.	open, honest, direct
Underling n.	master
Underneath prep.	above, top
Underrate adj.	overate

Understanding n.	ignorance **adj.** intolerant
Undertake vb.	achieve
Undervalue vb.	overestimate
Undersigned adj.	intentional
Undeveloped adj.	mature
Undisguised adj.	veiled
Unending adj.	brief, transient
Unequivocal adj.	ambiguous
Unerring adj.	faulty
Uneven adj.	flat, equal, regular
Uneventful adj.	eventful
Unexpected adj.	expected, predicted, anticipated
Unfaltering adj.	wavering
Unfamiliar adj.	familiar, versed
Unfathomable adj.	shallow
Unfeeling adj.	compassionate, sensitive
Unfledged adj.	experienced
Unforeseen adj.	expected
Ungainly adj.	graceful, dexterous
Ungodly adj.	pious, religious
Ungovernable adj.	mild
Unguarded adj.	protected, cautious
Unhappy adj.	happy, joyful, joyous
Unharmed adj.	hurt
Unhealthy adj.	healthy, salubrious, well, hale
Unhesitating adj.	wavering
Unholy adj.	devout, pious
Unidentified adj.	unknown

Uniform adj.	irregular
Unify vb.	separate
Uninteresting adj.	exciting, interesting, thrilling
Uninterrupted adj.	broken
Union n.	separation, discord
Unique adj.	common, ordinary, commonplace
Unite vb.	divide, separate, sever
Unity n.	discord
Universal adj.	local, regional, narrow
Unjust adj.	just, fair
Unlike adj.	similar
Unlikely adj.	likely, porbable
Unmanageable adj.	docile, handy
Unmannerly adj.	polite
Unmistakable adj.	doubtful
Unmoved adj.	moved, shaken
Unnecessary adj.	necessary, required
Unoccupied adj.	occupied
Unobtrusive adj.	pretentious
Unparalleled adj.	ordinary
Unpremeditated adj.	meditated, deliberate, planned
Unperturbed adj.	agitated
Unprincipled adj.	honest
Unrest n.	peace, tranquility
Unrighteous adj.	good, fair
Unruffled adj.	agitated

Unruly adj.	orderly
Unscathed adj.	hurt
Unscrupulous adj.	honest, principled
Unsettled adj.	settled, calm, placid
Unsightly adj.	beautiful, attractive
Unsolicited adj.	requested
Unsolicited adj.	requested
Unsound adj.	sound, stable, valid
Unsparing adj.	sparing, merciful, mean
Unspoken adj.	stated
Unstable adj.	stable, steady
Unsubstantial adj.	solid
Unsuccessful adj.	fruitful, successful
Unsung adj.	famous
Unsurpassed adj.	inferior
Unsuspecting adj.	suspicious
Untaught adj.	educated, taught
Unthinkable adj.	conceivable
Unthinking adj.	thoughtful
Untouched adj.	damaged, moved
Untroubled adj.	agitated
Untrue adj.	correct, faithful
Unused adj.	used, accustomed
Unusual adj.	usual
Unvarying adj.	changing
Unwarranted adj.	unsatisfied
Unwieldy adj.	handy
Unyielding adj.	flexible, yielding, compliant

Uphill adj.	easy, downhill
Uphold adj.	oppose
Uplift vb.	lower
Upright adj.	horizontal, dishonest
Uproar n.	peace, calm
Upset adj.	calm, composed
Upshot n.	beginning
Urbane adj.	uncouth, uncultivated
Urge vb.	dissuade, discourage, deter
Urgent adj.	unimportant
Use vb.	save, conserve
Vacant adj.	full, filled, occupied, bright, alert, intelligent

V

Vacation n.	term
Vacillating adj.	firm, steady
Vagrant adj.	settled
Vague adj.	specific, unequivocal, clear
Vain adj.	humble, worthwhile
Valiant adj.	cowardly
Valid adj.	weak, invalid
Valour n.	cowardice
Valuable adj.	worthless
Vanish vb.	appear
Vanity n.	modesty
Vanquish vb.	surrender

Variable adj.	constant, unwavering
Variegated adj.	plain
Variance n.	agreement
Variety n.	uniformity
Various adj.	identical
Vast adj.	small, tiny
Vegetable vb.	wither, shrivel
Vehement adj.	subdued
Veil vb.	expose
Velocity n.	Slowness
Venerate vb.	despise
Vengeance n.	forgiveness
Verbal adj.	written, printed
Verbose adj.	terse, reticent
Verify vb.	refute
Verity n.	falsity
Very adv.	slightly
Vest vb.	strip
Veteran adj.	novice
Veto n.	approval, consent **vb.** approve
Vex vb.	soothe, pacify, appease
Vice n.	virtue
Vicinity n.	distance
Vicious adj.	kind
Vicissitude n.	stability
Victor n.	loser
Victory n.	defeat
View vb.	ignore

Vigilant adj.	careless, negligent
Vigorous adj.	weak, lazy, lethargic, sluggish
Vile adj.	good
Villain n.	hero
Village n.	city, metropolis
Vivacious adj.	torpid
Vindictive adj.	forgiving
Violate vb.	observe, respect
Violent adj.	gentle
Virtual adj.	actual, real
Virtually adv.	actually
Virtue n.	vice
Virtuous adj.	wicked, evil, immoral
Virulent adj.	harmless, mild
Visible adj.	invisible
Vision n.	blindness
Visionary adj.	real
Vital adj.	unimportant
Vitality n.	weakness
Vitiate vb.	improve
Vivid adj.	vague, unclear
Vocal adj.	silent
Vociferous adj.	quiet
Voice n.	silence **vb.** suppress
Void adj.	valid
Volition n.	compulsion
Voluble adj.	reticent, taciturn
Voluminous adj.	small

Voluntary adj.	compulsory, required, forced
Volunteer vb.	withhold
Vulgar adj.	refined
Vulnerable adj.	tough

W

Waggish adj.	serious
Wail vb.	rejoice
Wait vb.	proceed, continue
Waive vb.	assert
Wake vb.	sleep, doze
Wander vb.	settle
Wane vb.	wax
Want n.	possession, abundance **vb.** possess
War n.	peace
Ward n.	guardian
Warlike adj.	pacific, peaceful
Warm adj.	cool, brisk, indifferent, cool
Warmth n.	coolness, apathy, coldness
Warp vb.	straighten
Wary adj.	careless, rash
Wash vb.	soil
Waste vb.	save, flourish
Wasteful adj.	economical

Watch vb.	ignore, neglect
Watchful adj.	heedless
Watery adj.	dry
Waver vb.	decide
Wayward adj.	docile
Weak adj.	strong, powerful
Weaken vb.	strengthen
Weakness n.	strength, aversion, dislike
Wealth n.	poverty, scarcity
Weary adj.	refreshed
Weather vb.	succumb
Weave vb.	unravel, destroy
Wed vb.	divorce
Weep vb.	rejoice, celebrate
Weigh vb.	relieve
Weighty adj.	light, trivial
Weird adj.	normal
Welcome adj.	unwelcome
Well adj.	bad, ill **adv.** badly
Wholly adv.	partly
Wicked adj.	good
Wide adj.	narrow, thin
Widen vb.	narrow
Widespread adj.	restricted
Wild adj.	restrained, tame
Wile adj.	artlessness
Willing adj.	reluctant, hesitant

Willingly adv.	reluctantly, hesitantly, wilt **vb.** thrive, flourish
Wily adj.	artless, simple, honest
Win vb.	lose, forfeit
Winner n.	loser
Winsome adj.	repulsive
Wisdom n.	folly
Wise adj.	foolish, foolhardy
Wit n.	stupidity
With prep.	without
Withdraw vb.	place, enter, remain
Withdrawn adj.	extrovert
Wither vb.	flourish, thrive
Withhold vb.	give
Withstand vb.	yield, give up
Witness vb.	miss
Woe n.	joy
Wonder n.	indifference
Wonderful adj.	ordinary
Work vb.	rest **n.** idleness
Worldly adj.	spiritual, unsophisticated
Worried adj.	calm
Worry vb.	delight, reassure
Worsen vb.	improve
Worship vb.	scorn
Worthless adj.	worthy
Worthy adj.	unworthy
Wrap vb.	unwrap

Wrath n.	composure
Wrathful adj.	pleased
Wreck vb.	build
Wretched adj.	fine, wonderful
Wrinkle vb.	smooth
Wrong adj.	right, correct, accurate, good, proper

Y

Yell vb.	whisper
Yellow adj.	brave, bold
Yield vb.	resist
Yielding adj.	stubborn, rigid
Yoke n.	freedom **vb.** release
Young adj.	old, mature, grown
Youngster n.	adult, grownup
Youthful adj.	old

Z

Zany adj.	serious
Zeal n.	apathy
Zealous adj.	apathetic
Zenith n.	nadir
Zest n.	insipidity, unenthusiasam
Zigzag adj.	straight